The bargain sector

African Studies Centre
Research Series
17/2001

The bargain sector

Economic restructuring and the non-farm sector in the Nigerian savanna

Kate Meagher

 Routledge
Taylor & Francis Group

LONDON AND NEW YORK

First published 2001 by Ashgate Publishing

Reissued 2018 by Routledge
2 Park Square, Milton Park, Abingdon, Oxon OX14 4RN
711 Third Avenue, New York, NY 10017, USA

Routledge is an imprint of the Taylor & Francis Group, an informa business

Publisher's Note
The publisher has gone to great lengths to ensure the quality of this reprint but points out that some imperfections in the original copies may be apparent.

Disclaimer
The publisher has made every effort to trace copyright holders and welcomes correspondence from those they have been unable to contact.

A Library of Congress record exists under LC control number: 2002421569

Photographs: Adamu Buba

Cover photo: Fulani women selling millet balls and sour milk (*fura da nono*)

ISBN 13: 978-0-415-79306-3 (hbk)
ISBN 13: 978-1-138-70161-8 (pbk)
ISBN 13: 978-1-315-20995-1 (ebk)

Contents

List of tables   *viii*
List of figures and plates   *ix*
Acknowledgements   *xi*
Preface   *xiii*

1. INTRODUCTION: THE STORY TO BE TOLD   *1*
   Conventional images and non-farm truths   *4*
   The restructuring of rural development policy   *6*
   From the general to the particular   *7*
   The case of the Nigerian savanna   *10*
   Shifting terms of reference   *13*

2. THE CHANGING ROLE OF THE RURAL NON-FARM SECTOR: ISSUES OF
   POLICY AND THEORY   *16*
   The policy issue   *17*
   Theoretical issues   *20*
   Historical perspectives: Non-farm activities and
   *   the rural economy in the Nigerian savanna*   *25*
   Theoretical perspectives of the 1960s and 1970s:
   *   Agricultural development and rural inequality*   *30*
   Perspectives of the 1980s and 1990s:
   *   The role of ecology, policy and economic restructuring*   *34*
   Quantitative evidence on trends in non-farm income
   *   shares, 1972-1993*   *37*

3. METHODOLOGY   *41*
   Nasarawan Doya: A village and a setting   *43*
   Research methodology   *46*
   Methodological problems   *50*

4. THE DETERMINANTS OF NON-FARM PARTICIPATION: HOUSEHOLD
    INEQUALITY AND AGRICULTURAL RESTRUCTURING   *53*
    The determinants of agricultural inequality   *55*
    Land: Equalizer or push factor?   *57*
    Inputs, crop prices and cropping choices   *62*
    Perceptions of agricultural constraints and prospects   *67*
    Pull factors: Household characteristics, non-farm participation
        and rural inequality   *70*

5. NON-FARM ACTIVITIES AND STRUCTURAL ADJUSTMENT:
    AN ENTERPRISE PERSPECTIVE   *78*
    The history of non-farm activities in Nasarawan Doya   *79*
    Current patterns of non-farm activities   *81*
    Labour and employment   *84*
    Sources of capital and credit   *86*
    Access to inputs and equipment   *89*
    Demand side factors: Competition and markets   *91*
    Incomes and income use   *93*
    New pressures and new opportunities in the non-farm sector   *94*

6. NON-FARM ACTIVITIES AND RURAL LIVELIHOOD STRATEGIES   *109*
    Patterns of participation in non-farm activities
        at the household level   *110*
    Non-farm livelihood strategies   *116*
    The importance of non-farm activities in total labour time   *118*
    Non-farm incomes as a share of household incomes   *121*
    Non-farm activities and agriculture: Investment patterns
        and occupational identities   *125*
    Migration patterns and non-farm options   *128*

7. HOUSEHOLD WELFARE AND SOCIAL NETWORKS:
   A NON-FARM PERSPECTIVE   *132*
   Household welfare and responsibilities for household
       provisioning   *133*
   Sources of women's non-farm capital   *135*
   Women's investment priorities   *138*
   Social networks and community associations   *139*

8. CONCLUSION   *145*
   Current trends in the role of the non-farm sector   *146*
   Long-term trends in non-farm income shares   *148*
   Future prospects for the non-farm sector:
       Theoretical issues and research concerns   *152*
   Policy reflections   *159*

Epilogue   *169*

Appendix   *171*

References   *173*

List of tables

2.1   Share of non-farm activities in total cash income in Rogo village,
        Nigeria, 1974/5–1992/3   *38*

4.1   Rural inequality and average levels of wet season agricultural production
        and sales, 1995/6   *56*
4.2   Average land holdings of households and household members   *58*
4.3   Women's land holdings and forms of tenure   *59*
4.4   Importance of various forms of land tenure   *60*
4.5   Price indices for fertilizer, grains and the rural cost of living, 1991-95   *64*
4.6   Percent share of major cash crops in total crop income   *65*
4.7   Aspects of household composition that influence access
        to non-farm incomes   *71*
4.8   Participation in non-farm activities   *73*
4.9   Household heads' perceptions of inter-generational accumulation of key
        economic assets   *74*

5.1   The composition of the enterprise sample   *82*
5.2   Labour use in non-farm enterprises   *85*
5.3   Sources of start-up capital for current non-farm enterprises   *87*
5.4   Inflation levels of major equipment, input and output costs
        between 1992 and 1997   *90*

6.1   Non-farm participation among household members   *111*
6.2   Seasonal participation (and non-participation) rates in non-farm activities among
        household members   *114*
6.3   Time spent on agricultural and non farm activities
        as a share of total working time   *119*
6.4   Relatives shares of household income sources, 1994-1996   *122*

A.1   Correlation of number of non-farm activities in household with age of head
        and labour ratio   *169*

List of figures and plates

Figures

8.1   Changes in non-farm income shares in the Nigerian savanna   *149*

Plates

1   Motorcycle taxis waiting for passengers in the village square   *101*
2   Fulani women selling millet balls and sour milk (*fura da nono*)   *102*
3   Local sugar producers: the sugar crushing machine and horse   *103*
4   Local sugar producers: boiling and moulding the sugar   *104*
5   Girls selling snacks for their secluded mothers   *105*
6   A provisions shop in Nasarawan Doya   *106*
7   Local blacksmith's working hut   *107*
8   Local blacksmiths making hoe holders   *108*

Acknowledgements

This study has been a true learning experience. Almost nothing went according to plan. But, as with all good learning experiences, the struggle has proven fruitful. It has provided an opportunity for unforseen rural realities to intrude themselves into my theoretical framework, with disorganizing, but edifying consequences. It has also provided an opportunity for me to experience the kindness and patience of the many people whose support made this study possible, with all its hitches. First and foremost, I would like to thank Deborah Bryceson of the Africa Studies Centre, Leiden, whose intellectual leadership and tireless fund-raising have helped to refocus empirical attention on the restructuring of African rural economies, and whose patience has seen so many of us through the long task of working through our findings. I would also like to acknowledge the generous assistance of the Dutch Ministry of Foreign Affairs, who funded the project. I owe more than gratitude to my tireless research assistant, Ibrahim Mohammed. His commitment to the orderly conduct of the fieldwork was both heartening and indispensable. Thanks are equally due to Rufa'i Mohammed, Lauratu Usman, Hauwa Abubakar, and Raikiya, not only for their efforts in the field, but for the comraderie they brought to the experience. For expert assistance with data entry and analysis, I am indebted to Danladi Jarma and Mr. Razak of the Institute for Agricultural Research, Ahmadu Bello University, Zaria.

The work would have been both slower and less thorough without the ready assistance of our many facilitators in Nasarawan Doya – Alh. Dauda, 'Prince' Abdullahi, and a range of others – and we benefited greatly from the gracious cooperation of the late Sarki of Nasarawan Doya, who, sadly, passed away some months after the conclusion of the fieldwork. Last, but not least, I owe the substance of what I have learned to the people of Nasarawan Doya, who put up so calmly and hospitably with our comings and goings, our long interviews, our endless rounds of questions – intrusions to which they have yielded so many times over the years, with little result. I thank them for their faith that, one day, something good may come of it.

I'm happy that the African Studies Centre, Leiden, decided to publish this manuscript in their Research Series. In particular, I want to thank Dick Foeken for his support and Mieke Zwart who did the layout.

Preface

Nigeria's large urban population and oil wealth have tended to deflect attention from its rural areas. Relative to many other Sub-Saharan African countries, rural non-farm activities are relatively under-researched in Nigeria. Kate Meagher's study of the savanna village of Nasarawan Doya is an important and timely contribution to this field. Her work indicates that the Nigerian peasantry have benefited comparatively little from the nation's oil wealth. The implementation of structural adjustment and economic liberalization policies, on the other hand, have had far-reaching consequences. Rural households have been differentially affected with many facing severe productive and welfare constraints.

This study builds on research findings emanating from the De-agrarianization and Rural Employment (DARE) research programme coordinated by the African Studies Centre, Leiden, and financed by the Netherlands Ministry of Foreign Affairs. The DARE programme involved four core research teams in Ethiopia, Nigeria, Tanzania and South Africa. Kate Meagher's study was linked to the work of her fellow DARE research team members, Abdul Raufu Mustapha, Mohamed-Bello Yunusa, Mohamed Iliya, and Barth Chukwuezi, based at the Centre for Research and Documentation, Kano.

The DARE programme's research programme objectives have been to compare and contrast the process of de-agrarianization in various rural areas of Africa in terms of economic activity reorientation, occupational adjustment, social identification, and spatial relocation of rural dwellers away from strictly peasant modes of livelihood. The extent and nature of non-agricultural activities in rural areas have been examined in relation to the influence of risk on rural household production and exchange. As has been amply demonstrated in the case of Nawarawan Doya, and mirrored in all the other DARE case study findings, de-agrarianization processes in Africa have in fact reaffirmed rather than undermined the importance of the 'subsistence fallback' – rural dwellers' reliance on own-farm produced staple foodstuffs.

The overall findings from the DARE programme are intended to provide insight into the processes of change which are moulding the livelihood prospects of African rural and urban dwellers in the twenty-first century. It is hoped that the knowledge gained may be useful for formulating more effective developmental policies to assist in short-circuiting Sub-Saharan Africa's current economic and political vulnerabilities.

Deborah Fahy Bryceson
DARE Research Programme Coordinator
African Studies Centre, Leiden

Introduction: The story to be told

The story began with the admission of the failure ... of industrialisation-led development strategies to generate income entitlements for the poor sufficiently fast and on a wide enough basis. Hopes were pinned on the new "bargain" sector, the rural non-farm economy. ...[However] the rural non-farm sector must not be viewed as a panacea for the fundamental problems of rural development and poverty alleviation. The problem of development is a problem of the whole; it cannot be solved by tinkering with a single part. (Saith 1992:113-114)

At the end of the dirt road leading into Nasarawan Doya, a Muslim Hausa village in the grain surplus region of the northern Nigerian savanna, there is a clearing that serves as a rendez-vous point for transport down to the main road, a tarred federal highway running between the state capitals of Kano and Kaduna. A red minibus, owned by a man from a village some 50km away, is normally parked there, waiting for a sufficient number of passengers to make the journey. At strategic times of day, a swarm of young men on motorcycles also wait for passengers going to the main road or out to the farms and hamlets along tracks too narrow for vehicles. In the shade of a small storehouse at the centre of the clearing, a line of young girls sell local snacks prepared by women from the village, the majority of whom pursue a range of non-agricultural activities from within the confines of the household, owing to the strict observation of the Islamic practice of wife seclusion.

To the left of the clearing as one enters the village is an abandoned dispensary which now serves as a police station for the lone police officer recently assigned to the village from the Local Government headquarters in the rural town of Makarfi. To the right stands the village's only bakery, owned by a local villager. The bakery has been abandoned since 1992 owing to the unmanageably high cost of flour resulting from Nigeria's imposition of a ban on imported wheat in 1986. In 1997, two young Igbo men from Imo State in south-eastern Nigeria rented the bakery and machinery, in the hope that the unbanning of wheat and rapidly rising transport costs to the nearest town have revived the demand for locally produced bread.

A commercial lodging, built like the village compounds around it of mud and cement with a traditional vaulted mud roof, stands at the far end of the clearing. One of the rooms is rented to a community health worker who works in the public clinic at the edge of the village. Two others are rented as a private clinic, opened during Nigeria's 1996 meningitis epidemic by a Yoruba nurse who works in a private hospital in Zaria, 35 km away. However, business has fallen off since end of the epidemic, leading to the temporary closure of the clinic for the rest of the year, and throughout the whole of 1997.

The commercial lodging is owned by a well-to-do villager who lives in the adjacent compound. In addition to wet and dry season farming and livestock holdings, this man earns significant additional income from rent, commercial operation of a grinding machine and the artisanal production of local sugar, for which he has acquired four horses and two sugarcane crushing machines. Three of his four secluded wives also bring in cash incomes from the production and sale of a range of local snacks, as well as seasonal crop trading. The fourth wife was obliged to abandon local snack production in 1996 when the marriage of her daughter deprived her of her sales agent. She now performs wage labour for the snack production enterprise of one of the other wives.

The frontage of the commercial lodging is whitewashed and zinc-roofed. A row of lock-up stalls run the length of it, with a chemist shop at the far end. The chemist is run by another young Igbo from Abia State, who came to northern Nigeria a few years ago to work in his brother's chemist in Tashin Yari, a village cum way station 10 km up the main road. They set up a chemist shop in Nasarawan Doya in 1995 as a branch of the main shop in Tashin Yari. The chemist is a favourite gathering point for the village youth, including one Yoruba from south-western Nigeria who opened a small provisions shop a couple of years ago and since then has been given land in the village to farm.

Old men normally gather for much of the day on the zinc-roofed porch beside the chemist while the able-bodied men are at the farm. In the mornings they buy breakfast porridge (*kunu*) and fried bean cakes (*kwosai*) from passing sales girls retailing their secluded mothers' wares. In the early afternoon, they buy *fura da nono*, a local midday meal of millet and soured milk sold by pastoral Fulani women from the outlying hamlets.

Another commercial lodging, a little deeper inside the village, is rented largely by single young men who work at the toll gate a few kilometres down the main road. The toll gate was previously federally owned, but was sold during a privatization exercise to a wealthy businessman from Nasarawan Doya, who currently resides in Zaria city. In 1997, he became the Local Government Chairman of Makarfi under the banner of General Sani Abacha's dubious (and later annulled) local government elections. He has since been made Village Head of Nasarawan Doya, as well as District Head of the newly created administrative district to which Nasarawan Doya belongs.

Nearby, a blacksmith works on agricultural implements, repairs bicycles, motorcycles and grinding machines, as well as producing bicycle seats for sale. He belongs to the only smithing family in Nasarawan Doya and all the surrounding villages, which has sustained demand for his services, but his earnings and capital have declined over the past decade owing to the increasing cost and scarcity of scrap metal. From his earnings as a blacksmith, he hires labour to farm for him, though he relies very little on farming for his livelihood.

During the wet season, men and youths drift in from the farm from mid-afternoon on. In addition to farming for themselves, many of the youths also engage in agricultural wage labour in the hope of building up capital to buy land, get married, and start up their own non-agricultural activity. The available pool of agricultural wage labour is further swelled by migrant labourers and Koranic students from the drier areas of Kano and Katsina State to the north, who come to the village to study with local scholars, and may be used on the farm by their teacher, or hired out to others. During the dry season, migrant labourers from southern Kaduna State drift into the village to find work on dry season farms.

Most of the local men pursue a range of non-farm activities, both within and outside the village. At the beginning of the dry season, the production and trading of local sugar, made in the form of small brown cakes from locally produced sugarcane, is currently one of the most lucrative activities, and is pursued at varying levels by at least one third of resident households. Since the imposition of structural adjustment, the rising price of imported sugar has created an expanding demand for local sugar in the rural as well as urban areas of northern Nigeria. A wide range of other activities are pursued, both seasonally, and, increasingly throughout the year. Those with some capital or technical skills engage in such activities as bicycle or radio repair, crop trading to regional markets and beyond, trade in a range of manufactured goods, mechanized food processing, or transport. Those with little capital engage in agricultural wage labour, load carrying, petty trade, manual food processing and a variety of traditional crafts ranging from local building to the embroidery of traditional caps.

Conventional images and non-farm truths

Diversification into a range of non-farm activities is nothing new in Nasarawan Doya, nor in northern Nigeria as a whole. In the semi-arid environment of the northern guinea savanna, the rural economy has for centuries involved the interdependence of agricultural and non-farm activities. This is not because the local agricultural system is unproductive;

in fact, Nasarawan Doya lies within a traditionally food surplus region which has developed a relatively successful and highly commercialized peasant agriculture. But food surplus agriculture, combined with a short and somewhat unreliable growing season, have generated the need, the resources and the trading contacts for the development of a wide variety of non-agricultural income sources. Most of these were traditionally pursued during the long dry season, but they have also been drawn upon in times of inadequate rainfall or as a means of investing surplus resources.

Ecological and economic changes over the past three decades have tended to intensify the importance of the non-farm sector in rural livelihood strategies. Although not plagued by drought like the sahel savanna to the north, Nigeria's northern guinea savanna has experienced increasingly unreliable rainfall patterns since the early 1970s, which have increased the need to rely on non-farm sources of income to make up for deficits in crop production.[1] Furthermore, the introduction and wide-spread uptake of chemical inputs, especially fertilizers, has intensified the need for cash during the course of the growing season. These developments, combined with broader trends of commercialization in agricultural production processes and rapid inflation of the cost of living, have fuelled the expansion of the non-farm sector from a dry season to a year round phenomenon.

The central role of non-farm activities in the food surplus areas of the Nigerian savanna challenges the conventional wisdom regarding the non-farm sector in Africa. First of all, it challenges the image of rural Africa as predominantly agrarian. A recent comparative study by Reardon et al. (1998) indicates that non-farm incomes account for an average of 42% of the total incomes of rural African households. In fact, Africa shows a higher average share of non-farm incomes than either Asia or Latin America. While a high proportion of Africans still live in the rural areas, their livelihoods are less agricultural than in any other developing region.

Secondly, there is a tendency to view a heavy dependence on non-farm activities as characteristic of agriculturally unproductive regions. However,

---

[1] The guinea savanna will henceforward be referred to simply as the 'savanna', except in cases where there is need to distinguish it from the sahel savanna, now conventionally referred to as the 'drylands'.

literature on agricultural growth linkages has argued for some years that the rural non-farm sector grows fastest in areas where agriculture is dynamic (Hazell and Haggblade 1991; Reardon et al. 2000). In unfavourable agro-climatic zones, households access a significant proportion of non-farm incomes through migration to towns or to agriculturally more dynamic areas where higher returns from agriculture generate a greater availability of non-farm employment (Reardon et al. 1998). The conventional association of rural non-farm activities with unproductive or high risk agriculture is a bias created more by policy makers than by empirical realities. Until recently, policy makers were largely uninterested in rural non-farm activities in areas where agriculture had the potential to provide a sufficient livelihood.

The restructuring of rural development policy

While non-farm incomes have been economically important in rural Africa for centuries, two recent developments have triggered a dramatic upsurge in policy interest in the non-farm sector. The first is the impact on rural economies of economic restructuring, embodied in structural adjustment programmes and the economic pressures of globalization. These forces have generated a range of new pressures and new opportunities within the rural economy which appear to have intensified recourse to non-farm incomes. While hard evidence remains sketchy, some studies have pointed to an increase in the share of non-farm incomes in total household incomes across a range of African countries (Bryceson 1997; Reardon et al. 1998). Such observations have been accompanied by evidence of a proliferation of non-farm activities in rural areas. This apparent expansion of the non-farm sector at a time of generalized economic contraction has caught the attention of orthodox economists and policy makers.

A second development which has further intrigued the policy orthodoxy is that the evidence of non-farm sector growth coincides with the emergence of a serious gap in rural development policy. Structural adjustment has severely curtailed public sector agricultural support programmes. At the same time, the liberalization of input and output markets has failed to attract sufficient private sector involvement to fill the gap left by state withdrawal. In a burst of often unfounded optimism, neo-liberal ideologues and policy makers have seized upon the rural non-farm sector as a potentially dynamic new source of rural income support and funding for agricultural investment. Since 1998, the World Bank has initiated a programme of policy and investment work in the rural non-farm sector, and has entered into a major collaborative research programme with the UK Department for International Development (DFID) focusing on policies for the development of the rural non-farm sector. Over the same period, an issue with a special focus on the rural non-farm sector has been put out by the FAO journal, *The State of Food and Agriculture, 1998*, and a heavy concentration of articles on the non-farm sector is planned for a forthcoming issue of *World Development*.

From the general to the particular

Amidst the tangle of conventional images of rural Africa and new policy 'spins', the nature and developmental role of the rural non-farm sector remain poorly understood, despite the recent flurry of research on the subject. The core of the problem lies in the tendency to focus on global economic forces and structural adjustment policies as the main forces of change in rural Africa, and on quantitative indicators as the main features of those changes. This tends to gloss over the decisive role of local factors. As Luis Llambi (2000: 189) argues in the context of Latin America, it is important

> ... to emphasize the links between globalization processes, structural adjustment programmes and contemporary rural restructuring, but this only makes sense when accompanied by a deep historical knowledge of these changes focusing on what is old and what is new in each case study.

In a region such as Africa, which is characterized by an astonishing level of agro-ecological and ethnic diversity – not to mention wide variations in pre-colonial and colonial history, political systems and popular economic institutions – comparatively uniform forces of structural adjustment and globalization must necessarily have widely varying impacts on rural society. These cannot be effectively analysed on the basis of broad economic trends averaged across several countries. On the other hand, detailed local studies contribute relatively little to current debates unless they are situated within the context of broader regional, continental and global trends. The current tendency to achieve the linkage between the particular and the general by focusing only on what can be quantified has led to a heavy emphasis on internationally comparable data, but with very limited understanding of the meaning of observed trends, or of the social mechanisms that regulate them.

What is needed is a more holistic approach to the analysis of the non-farm sector. The issue of holism needs to be addressed at three levels: the types of data collected, the determinants of change identified, and the analysis of the impact of economic and policy change in the non-farm sector on other facets of rural economy and society. Regarding types of data, it is important to combine both qualitative and quantitiative approaches in non-farm sector research. An understanding of the factors governing trends in the non-farm sector depends on the ability to go beyond the computation of sectoral linkages and income shares, by situating these economic features of non-farm participation within the historical and social context which has shaped them. Non-farm activities are not just reciprocals of agricultural participation, but economic pursuits with distinct histories and widely varying technical, skill and capital requirements. Similarly, inhabitants of a given rural area are not Marx's proverbial 'sack of potatoes', but actors who may come from varying ethnic and religious backgrounds, and possess different levels of capital, education and skills, not to mention variations in gender and status within the household – all of which influence the extent and types of non-farm participation. Despite increasing attention to issues of gender and socio-economic status, an appreciation of the range of factors that influence access to non-farm activities is often blocked by prevalent assumptions of ethnic homogeneity within African villages, and an extremely one-sided analysis of the effects of migration, which focuses on the movement of locals, but ignores the possibility of in-migrants from other areas.

Greater sensitivity to local factors also involves a more differentiated analysis of the factors influencing trends in non-farm growth. Over-emphasis on global forces of economic restructuring has distracted attention from a range of local factors which differentiate rather than homogenize patterns of rural diversification. Ann Gordon (1999) has pointed to the need to develop rural economy typologies that could provide pointers to appropriate types of policy interventions in different areas. While Reardon et al. (1998) have taken a stab at continent-wide typologies of non-farm development based on levels of rural-urban integration, more intra-regionally sensitive variables are needed for an understanding of the complex of agro-economic and institutional factors governing rural diversification strategies in different areas. These include such factors as local land availability (not individual access but general conditions of land shortage or land surplus), cash-cropping systems (food-crop vs export crop), characteristic migration patterns (ranging from permanent out-migration to seasonal in-migration), and the nature of indigenous economic and cooperative institutions (trading networks, credit groups, development associations, etc.). In the existing non-farm literature, these factors are either ignored or are treated as household- or individual-level variables rather than as typological elements of non-farm change.

A final aspect in which a local perspective contributes to greater holism relates to the understanding of the overall dynamic of the rural economy and the ways in which it is affected by changes in the non-farm sector. Current research efforts have placed a heavy emphasis on thematic and comparative studies, which isolate the non-farm dimension and illustrate its links with the rest of the economy through an array of examples drawn from a vast range of countries. The disadvantage (or advantage, depending on one's objectives) of this approach is that potentially negative side-effects of key economic and policy changes never become apparent. The positive impact of non-farm incomes on agricultural investment is illustrated with an example from Kenya; their positive impact on poverty is highlighted by examples from the Sahel, and the positive impact of adjustment policies on non-farm growth is backed up by anecdotes from small rural towns in Zimbabwe. The issue policy-makers should be addressing, however, is how the growth of non-farm-stimulated agricultural investment in a given rural area affects the livelihoods of all strata of rural households, and how adjustment policies have affected both non-farm and agricultural incomes of better-off as well as poor households *in that same area*. In short, the real question concerns the complex interaction between agro-economic potential, social structure, economic change and policy regimes, taken as an interconnected dynamic rather than as a menu of isolable sectors, social groups and policy options. The sometimes exhaustively indepth study undertaken here represents an effort to bring these complex interactions to the fore, and to highlight the fact that side-effects, however unintended, are, in fact, effects with real repercussions.

The case of the Nigerian savanna

The Nigerian savanna was selected as the site for this study with a view to challenging some of the presuppositions and generalizations evident in current non-farm literature. These relate to the association of non-farm participation with poverty, and assumptions about the impact of structural adjustment, education, gender, and rural credit institutions on patterns of non-farm participation. Despite a comparatively high level of non-farm participation, the Nigerian guinea savanna represents, as mentioned above, an agricultural surplus zone with a relatively commercialized peasant agriculture. The main cash crops in the area are food crops, which, in contrast to export crops, have tended to benefit rather less from structural adjustment policies. Although the savanna displays a high level of differentiation in access to non-farm activities, education plays very little role in this process, and educational levels are uniformly low. Moreover, in contrast to conventional analyses of African agriculture, women in this area have relatively little involvement in agricultural production owing to the heavy influence of Islam on gender relations. To further compound the assault on conventional wisdom, village-level cooperative institutions are either weak or non-existent in this area, owing to a long pre-colonial history of integration into hierarchical guild and state systems.

Using these parameters, the village of Nasarawan Doya was selected as representative of the savanna region. As such, it is not a special case, but a location typical of conditions in a cultural and agro-ecological milieu that frames the lives of over 10 million rural inhabitants in Nigeria. The grain surplus savanna is, moreover, of strategic importance in Nigeria, and indeed in West Africa as a whole. Grain from this region plays a key role in food security throughout the country, and in several neighbouring West African states as well (Egg & Igue 1993; Meagher & Ogunwale 1994). The savanna region is also a centre of political and economic tensions between the Hausa-Fulani indigenes and more educationally advantaged ethnic groups from southern Nigeria – tensions which have increasingly serious implications for national stability. Given its implications for economic political stability over such a large area, getting things right on the non-farm sector matters a great deal in this region.

Unfortunately, optimistic assessments of the developmental potential of the non-farm sector do not appear to be borne out in the case of Nasarawan Doya. While the role of non-farm activities in local livelihood and accumulation strategies has changed significantly in the decade and a half since the imposition of Nigeria's Structural Adjustment Programme in 1986, the changes have been more negative than positive. At first glance, the statistics appear to suggest a dynamic process of income diversification. Dramatic increases in cash-crop prices since the late 1980s have been accompanied by high levels of diversification. Non-farm income shares in the village were found to average 60%[2] in 1996/7. But evidence of declining access to agricultural inputs and declining welfare indicators among the bulk of the population tell a different story. Rather than a story of mutually reinforcing accumulation, linkages between the farm and non-farm sectors have confronted most of the inhabitants of Nasarawan Doya with a scenario of mutually reinforcing impoverishment.

The driving force behind these negative developments is that, since the early 1990s, rising agricultural output prices have been outstripped by

---

[2] This figure includes income from agricultural wage labour.

increases in the price of key inputs, resulting in declining terms of trade in food crop agriculture. This has not only reduced input use, but intensified dependence on non-farm incomes for meeting household needs as well as input costs. To make matters worse, the economic pressures of structural adjustment have also undermined the profitability of the bulk of non-farm activities, which have also been plagued by rising input and equipment costs, and increasingly saturated rural markets. The few lucrative non-farm opportunities that have emerged under structural adjustment have tended to require relatively high levels of capital or skills. This restricts the exploitation of these opportunities to wealthier strata of rural households and more skilled migrants from other parts of Nigeria, intensifying levels of rural and regional inequality.

A central question underlying the present study is whether the changes currently taking place in Nasarawan Doya simply represent modern variations of the age-old practice of combining agricultural and non-farm activities to stabilize or improve livelihoods, or a trend toward an overall decline in the importance of agriculture in the rural economy of northern Nigeria. Growing evidence of a movement away from agriculturally-based livelihoods in rural Africa – a process recently labelled 'de-agrarianization' (Bryceson 1996) – raises important questions about the causal factors underlying such a trend, as well as the economic potential of the activities replacing agriculture as the central source of rural livelihoods. Thus, if the first question is whether de-agrarianization is indeed taking place in Nasarawan Doya, the second question revolves around the developmental implications of this process, both at the level of individual and household livelihood strategies, and at the wider sectoral and regional levels.

Other key questions to be raised revolve around the determinants of access to non-farm activities. How do household and individual characteristics, including access to land and capital, education, skills, ethnicity, and gender, affect access to non-farm activities? What is the impact of the non-farm sector on rural income inequality? Are inequalities in non-farm incomes governed by the same factors that determine inequalities in agricultural incomes?

The groundwork for this study will be set by an exploration of the general theoretical and policy issues relating to the African non-farm sector and its implications for agricultural and rural development. This will be further contextualized through a review of the historical and theoretical literature on the role of the non-farm sector in northern Nigeria. The empirical core of the study will then be introduced with a description of the village setting and the research methodology. The subsequent presentation and analysis of the research findings is divided into five parts. The first will consider the changes in the agricultural economy of the village which have influenced the development of the non-farm sector. This will be followed by a consideration, from an enterprise perspective, of the impact of structural adjustment on the development of the non-farm sector. The analysis will then shift to a household and community perspective to look at the role of non-farm activities in village livelihood strategies and occupational identities. In the following section, attention will turn to the role of non-farm activities in household welfare strategies, and the wider role of social networks in the development of the non-farm sector. Finally, a concluding section will attempt to draw out the theoretical, empirical and policy implications of the study.

Shifting terms of reference

Before moving into the study, critical terminological and definitional issues need to be addressed. Literature on non-farm activities goes back at least to the 1960s in Africa, and has involved a range of terms and definitions. Common terms include 'off-farm', 'non-farm', 'non-agricultural' and 'rural income diversification'. These terms have been treated as essentially interchangeable. Authors of 'non-farm' studies refer to data from 'off-farm' studies for comparative purposes or to illustrate changes over time (Liedholm 1973; Reardon et al. 1998). Although these terms appear to refer to the same facet of the rural economy, they actually arise from very different conceptual backgrounds. The terms 'non-agricultual' and 'non-farm' arise from a sectoral perspective on rural economic change. The 'non-farm' sector involves sources of rural income outside agriculture, and specifically excludes agricultural wage labour (Ellis 1998; Liedholm 1973; Byerlee et al. 1977). The major policy concern underpinning the term is the development of alternative rural incomes outside of agriculture to absorb rural labour and stem migration.

The terms 'off-farm' and 'rural income diversification' by contrast arise from a household perspective on rural economic change. The central concern is not whether the activities concerned are agricultural or non-agricultural in nature, but the fact that they take place outside the economic realm of the household farm. Norman defines 'off-farm' activities as 'occupations other than working on the family farm'. The key concerns are the extent to which such activities either draw key resources out of household agriculture, or increase income security and agricultural investment. Both 'off-farm' and 'rural income (or livelihood) diversification' include agricultural wage labour as an important dimension of income generation outside of household agriculture (Norman 1973b; Matlon 1979; Ellis 1998).

Increased policy interest in the non-farm sector, and a scramble for data from which to deduce trends in non-farm growth, have resulted in the virtual obliteration of these distinctions. Sectoral models appear to have triumphed, and 'non-farm' is now the reigning term, but many of the policy concerns and the data of the 'off-farm' and 'diversification' literature have been retained. The result is that agricultural wage labour, one of the most critical factors in the analysis of rural economic change, has been left in a sectoral limbo between the on-farm and the non-farm.[3]

In conformity with current usage, this study will adopt the term 'non-farm', but the term will be defined to include agricultural wage labour, for two reasons. The first is to permit effective comparisons with available northern Nigeria data from the 1960s and 1970s, which includes agricultural

---

[3] This post-shifting in the definition of the 'non-farm' is likely to compromise the comparability of income share data from the 1960s and 1970s with that of the 1980s and 1990s (Reardon et al. 1998: 291). Use of such data to support claims about long-term trends in the share of non-farm incomes in total rural incomes should be undertaken, and read, with caution.

wage labour under the rubric 'off-farm'. The second is because of the structural importance of agricultural wage labour in diversification out of household agriculture, particularly among the rural poor and rural youth. Thus, this study defines as non-farm any activities not concerned with the direct production of crops or livestock on personal or household farms, or with the direct realization of incomes from those activities. Selling ones own crops in the market is counted as agricultural income, but selling someone else's crops would count as non-farm income. Similarly, selling ones own sugarcane counts as agricultural income, while processing it into local sugar and selling it would be counted as non-farm income.

A final terminological issue relates to the question of whether the economic realm of non-farm activities should be referred to as a 'sector' or an 'economy'. Although 'rural non-farm economy' (RNFE) is currently favoured in work being conducted under the auspices of the World Bank, the term 'non-farm sector' has been chosen for this study in order to avoid the economic dualism implicit in the term 'non-farm economy'. While distinguished from agricultural activities, however fuzzily, the developmental potential of the non-farm sector is critically dependent on the fortunes of agriculture, and *vice versa*. The non-farm sector does not constitute a separate economy capable of exerting an independent influence on rural development; it is only a sector within, and inseparable from, the wider rural economy.

2

The changing role of
the rural non-farm sector:
Issues of policy and theory

The failure of the industrialization model of economic development, and the subsequent rise of structural adjustment processes, have provoked a significant conceptual shift in studies of the rural non-farm sector in Africa. The original focus of such studies was on surplus labour absorption and poverty alleviation for the landless and land poor (World Bank 1978; Byerlee et al. 1977). In the context of economic restructuring, however, non-farm incomes are seen to play a critical role not only for the rural poor, but for all categories of African rural producers. This new perspective on the non-farm sector has been triggered by growing evidence of a significant increase in diversification into non-agricultural activities at all levels of rural society, and a substantial, if not rising, share of non-farm incomes in the total income of rural households (Liedholm et al. 1994; Reardon 1997; Berry 1989). The apparent expansion of the rural non-farm sector, and its growing importance in rural livelihood strategies, has led to a consideration of its potential not only for increasing rural incomes, but as a stimulus for agricultural investment and rural enterprise development (Bryceson 1996; Delgado et al. 1994; Ellis 1998; Haggblade et al. 1989).

These observations and prospects have begun to coalesce around a policy agenda that accords the rural non-farm sector a more central role in the rural development process. However, the emerging policy perspective has taken on a strong ideological character that has tended to gloss over some of the critical problems of rural non-farm development in the African context. A serious consideration of the developmental prospects of the non-farm sector requires a more careful assessment of existing debates on its developmental capacity and socio-economic impact. This must begin with an outline of the emerging policy perspective, and then turn to an assessment of the main theoretical trends and issues of rural non-farm development in sub-Saharan Africa.

The policy issue

The reassessment of the economic importance and developmental potential of the non-farm sector arises from a number of structural shifts that have accompanied the African experience of structural adjustment. On the supply side, two factors come to the fore. First is the widespread shift from labour to land constraints in African agriculture, not only in high potential areas, but also in the semi-arid regions of Africa (Bryceson 1996; Matlon 1991; Reardon 1997). Secondly, rising unemployment and falling real incomes in the urban economy may be encouraging a trend toward return migration from the urban back to the rural areas. It has been hypothesized that return migrants are likely to bring with them higher levels of skills, education and capital which may encourage rural enterprise development, particularly in the context of a growing land constraint (Bryceson 1996; Reardon 1997).

On the demand side, it is argued that structural adjustment policies favour a reorientation of rural demand in favour of the rural non-farm sector, owing to the rising cost of imported and urban goods and services. In the context of liberalized crop prices, this was expected to involve the re-direction of an increasingly buoyant rural purchasing power. Devaluation, price liberalization and the removal of protective measures favouring large-scale industry have reduced access to imported and local industrial goods, creating a market for the products of rural small-scale enterprise, not only among the rural poor, but across the spectrum of rural society. In addition, cutbacks in state expenditure have reduced access to a range of rural infra-structural and social services, such as water, healthcare and education, opening up new opportunities for private entrepreneurs willing to provide these services (Bryceson 1996; Lanjouw 1999; World Bank 1989). Studies of non-farm growth linkages indicate that rural demand for locally produced goods and services accounts for approximately 80% of non-farm growth in African economies (Haggblade et al. 1989). This suggests that the expected reorientation of rural demand could provide a powerful stimulus to the growth of the rural non-farm sector.

Interest in the non-farm sector has been further stimulated by the possibility that it may fill a gap in agricultural investment created by structural adjustment. The withdrawal of the state from critical aspects of agricultural development, including input provision, credit, tractor services and input subsidies, has created the need for a new source of investible funds for agriculture. A number of recent studies have pointed to the non-farm economy as a critical source of funds for agricultural investment (Reardon et al. 1992; Delgado et al. 1994; Evans & Ngau 1991). Reardon et al. (1998: 330) directly link the context of state withdrawal from agricultural support services to the need for non-farm incomes to generate resources for agricultural investment:

> In many countries to date, private sector activity in the areas of input supply and credit has not emerged sufficiently to fill the gap left by government's withdrawal. Farmers are often forced to rely on own-cash sources of off-farm employment and cash cropping to pay for inputs and substitute for credit.

The overall policy thrust of the non-farm-centred perspective revolves around liberalization, labour-absorbing public works and infrastructural development, with a particular focus on rural road networks and the improvement of productive and marketing infrastructure in rural towns (Bryceson 1996; Ellis 1998; Reardon et al 1998; Lanjouw 1999). The basic idea is to remove the constraints to rural enterprise development in order to facilitate the capacity of rural dwellers to take advantage of the new opportunities opened up by the reorientation of supply and demand taking place under structural adjustment.

A number of problematic issues are raised by this approach. The first issue concerns whether a shift of developmental focus from agriculture to the non-farm sector is justified by the nature of the changes observed in the structure of the rural economy and its linkages with the wider economy. Is there adequate evidence of a significant long-term shift in household livelihood strategies in favour of non-farm sources of income? Does evidence of a proliferation of non-farm activities, or their rising share in total incomes, denote an increasing dynamism in the non-farm sector, or an increasing recourse to low-income survival activities in the context of instability in the agricultural economy? Can the growth potential of the non-farm sector be fostered without first ensuring the basic requirements of agricultural growth?

A second issue concerns whether liberalization and improved rural infrastructure – in short, the provision of free market conditions in the rural areas – are sufficient to promote economic growth within the non-farm sector, particularly under conditions of economic instability and contraction within the wider agricultural and industrial economies of most African countries. Issues such as the sources of capital for non-farm activities, the development of appropriate technical skills, and the nature of the activities and employment generated by these measures need to be addressed more specifically. The current portrayal of the rural non-farm sector is uncomfortably similar to that of the urban informal sector, with its attendant propensity to become a receptacle for a wide range of entrepreneurial virtues despite a glaring lack of the technical, financial and demand conditions for a free-market take-off.

A third issue concerns the question of who are likely to benefit from a shift in the rural development focus from agriculture to the rural non-farm sector. Who are best placed to take advantage of the new non-farm opportunities generated by structural adjustment? Is this likely to increase or to reduce income inequality in the rural areas? Whatever the impact on equity, the general assumption is that the beneficiaries of opportunities within the non-farm sector will be drawn from within rural society, either from the ranks of resident members of rural communities, or migrants forced to return to their rural homes by the downturn in the urban economy. Little consideration is given to the possibility that actors from outside the social and economic context of rural communities may move in on whatever new opportunities open up in the non-farm economy. This possibility is amplified by the policy emphasis on the development of road networks and the focus on infrastructural and activity clustering in small rural towns. The social, political and developmental implications of this possibility must be considered.

Theoretical issues

In addition to reshaping rural development policy, the structural changes identified above have reoriented the literature on the rural non-farm sector and its relationship to processes of economic change. Studies conducted during the 1960s and 1970s saw labour as the critical constraint on economic development in rural Africa, and tended to regard agricultural wage labour, urban migration and trade as the only structurally significant sources of non-farm incomes (Reardon 1997). Other forms of non-farm activities were regarded as relatively marginal, off-season endeavours, with limited implications for rural development and social change. The core debate was between those who felt that non-farm incomes contributed to agricultural development, by generating incomes in the off-season and contributing to agricultural intensification, and those who argued that involvement in non-farm activities drew critical labour out of agriculture and undermined the rural social structure.

Evidence of an emerging land constraint in many parts of sub-Saharan Africa, coupled with evidence of the growing importance of non-farm activities in rural livelihoods, has shifted the centre of gravity of the non-farm debate from whether it impedes agricultural development, to the nature of its developmental role in agricultural, and more generally rural, development.

The dominant perspective in the non-farm literature is represented by work on agricultural growth linkages. Represented by such authors as Delgado, Hazell, Haggblade and Reardon, this perspective recognizes in the non-farm sector a potential for income stabilization, poverty alleviation, and the generation of additional resources for agricultural investment. However, this stream of literature maintains staunchly that agricultural growth is the essential basis for any productive expansion of the non-farm sector (Haggblade et al. 1989; Delgado et al. 1994; Reardon et al. 1992). The non-farm sector is found to be less dynamic in Africa than in Asia, owing largely to the low technical level of agriculture, the sparseness and relative inaccessibility of the rural market, and the consequent lack of linkages between non-farm activities and large-scale industry (Bagachwa & Stewart 1992; Reardon et al. 1998). Haggblade et al. (1989) point to consumer demand generated by rising agricultural incomes as the central stimulus to non-farm growth in sub-Saharan Africa. However, the relatively sanguine assessment of the responsiveness of the African non-farm sector rests on excessively liberal definitions of what constitutes locally produced goods and services, and a tendency to gloss over the additional investment required to translate increased consumer demand into a supply response (Harriss 1987).

A second pro-non-farm perspective focuses on the capacity of the non-farm sector to take a *leading* rather than a complementary role in agricultural growth. Non-agricultural incomes are seen to provide resources which help households overcome the risks and capital constraints of agricultural investment and innovation (Evans & Ngau 1991; Tiffen et al. 1994). While most of the empirical studies of non-farm-led agricultural growth show a heavy dependence on remittances from urban employment, which are likely to falter in the context of structural adjustment, complementary trends in the literature focus on the dynamism of rural non-farm enterprises even under current economic conditions. This involves a range of relatively recent and often interlinked perspectives, principally those of 'de-agrarianization' (Bryceson 1996; Bryceson & Jamal 1997), and the literature on the developmental role of small rural towns (Rasmussen et al. 1992; Bryceson 1996; Bryceson & Jamal (ed.) 1997; Baker & Pedersen (eds.) 1992). These new perspectives emphasise the central role of small-scale rural enterprise in the economic restructuring of rural Africa. In particular, the small rural town literature addresses concerns expressed in the literature on growth linkages that African non-farm development is held back by the sparseness of its economic infrastructure and urban linkages. It is argued that small rural towns have become poles of rural entrepreneurial growth capable of fostering a dense network of economic and infrastructural linkages with village-based non-farm enterprises.

Interestingly, the two main streams in the pro-non-farm literature – the 'agricultural growth linkages' and the 'de-agrarianization/small rural town' perspectives – represent completely opposite perspectives on rural-urban relations and the fate of African agriculture. The literature on growth linkages regards increased links with urban industry as the key to African non-farm sector take-off (Reardon et al. 1998). By contrast, the small rural town approach argues that the entrepreneurial potential of the rural non-farm sector has been liberated by the eclipse of urban industry under structural adjustment (Pedersen 1997; Bryceson 1996). Similarly, the growth linkages perspective sees the non-farm sector as playing a vital role in sustaining the viability of African agriculture. By contrast, the de-agrarianization perspective presents the non-farm sector as providing an *alternative* to agricultural livelihoods, which are seen as economically doomed by the intensifying pressures of structural adjustment and the globalization of agricultual markets (Bryceson 2000). This second point of contrast gives a post-industrial twist to the Chayanovian and Marxist perspectives on the fate of the peasantry. What is particularly striking is that, unlike their 19th and 20th century counterparts, these diametrically opposed positions on the fate of African agriculture have not generated any direct debate. This is due largely to the fact that, in true post-Cold War fashion, they agree on the central policy issue: the promotion of the non-farm sector as a lynch pin of rural development. The bulk of the debate concerning the role of the non-farm sector has taken place largely at the margins, in the context of case studies and commentaries that question the optimistic assessments of the pro-non-farm literature in all its guises.

This more critical, and highly diverse, trend in the literature argues that the expanding role of the non-farm sector is due neither to agricultural growth nor to any new-found dynamism of rural non-farm enterprise. Current trends toward increased diversification are seen to represent survival strategies in the context of increasing agricultural instability and economic crisis. A wide range of studies highlight the vulnerability of rural households to the macro-shocks of adjustment, which have undermined rural incomes in many African countries, as well as disrupting vital linkages between the rural and urban economies (Jamal & Weeks 1993; Heyer 1996; Sahn & Sarris 1991). The expansion of the non-farm sector is seen to consist primarily in the proliferation of survival strategies which, at best, stave off further decline, and at worst, exert an adverse effect on agricultural investment and rural incomes (Berkvens 1997; Berry 1989, 1993a; Liedholm et al 1994). Attention is also drawn to the adverse effects of crisis and adjustment on supply-side factors of rural non-farm enterprises, and to the intensifying demand constraints affecting markets for many rural goods and services (Meagher & Mustapha 1997; Murton 1999).

A lack of consensus regarding the role of the non-farm sector in African rural development is accompanied by disagreements over the impact of the non-farm incomes on rural inequality. Some commentators argue that evidence regarding the impact of non-farm incomes on rural inequality shows no consistent pattern. They point out that, at the very least, the role of non-farm incomes in poverty alleviation dampens rural inequality (Bagachwa & Stewart 1992; Matlon 1979). However, this position is losing ground in the face of a wide range of studies indicating that in Africa, unlike Asia or Latin America, non-farm earnings are associated with an increase in rural inequality (Haggblade et al. 1989; Reardon 1997; Reardon et al. 2000; Saith 1992). Ellis (2000) points out that reducing the intensity of poverty at the lower end does not mean that the rural non-farm sector has an equalizing effect on rural incomes. Wealthier households across a range of African countries are found to have a higher share of non-farm income in total income, as well as higher absolute non-farm earnings, suggesting that, whatever the poor gain from diversification, the wealthy gain more. This has drawn attention to the role of barriers to entry in the distribution of non-farm income. Dercon & Krishnan (1996) found comparative advantage a more important determinant of diversification than risk aversion, advantaging households with greater access to particular skills, labour or capital, while channelling poorer households into easy access, low-return activities which do not contribute to improved consumption or asset holding. According to Sahn & Sarris (1991) and Reardon et al. (2000), economic restructuring is likely to exacerbate the negative impact of the non-farm sector on African rural inequality, owing to its tendency to lower returns to labour and increase barriers to entry.

The issue of unequal distribution of returns to non-farm participation has generated an awareness that diversification out of agriculture may be motivated by divergent factors with differing developmental implications. These have been characterized variously as 'push' and 'pull' factors (Gordon 1999; Reardon et al. 1998), 'survival' and 'accumulation' strategies (Hart 1994), or diversification by 'necessity' and by 'choice' (Ellis 2000). While sectoral perspectives have tended to concentrate on 'pull' factors, such as risk diversification and the quest for higher returns, there has been a growing recognition in this camp that 'push' factors are also significant. With reference to studies in Asia, Gordon (1999) has noted that poor households tend to diversify into activities where returns are no better than in agriculture, while better-off households are more likely to diversify into sectors that improve their returns. Conversely, household-based perspectives have tended to be more aware of the importance of 'push' factors, and of the socio-economic divide between 'push' and 'pull' factors (Davies 1996).

This survey of the non-farm literature raises a number of key issues to be investigated in the case study that follows. The first concerns the role of agriculture in the development of the non-farm sector. What are the factors within the agricultural sector that propel the expansion of the non-farm sector? Can the non-farm sector generate rural growth even in the context of agricultural decline?

The second key issue concerns whether current trends in non-farm sector expansion represent productive growth or unproductive proliferation of non-farm activities. An answer to this question requires an analysis of the impact of economic restructuring on supply-side conditions of non-farm activities. It also requires an empirical investigation of the impact of restructuring on demand for non-farm goods and services. Is demand expanding in the face of rising prices of urban alternatives, or is it contracting as a result of declining agricultural incomes? Since not all activities will be affected in the same way, it is important to identify any 'new opportunities' being generated by the restructuring process, and to consider whether access to these more profitable activities is evenly distributed.

The third issue relates to the impact of the non-farm sector on rural economic inequality. Does the non-farm sector counteract or reinforce patterns of rural inequality? How has economic restructuring affected the impact of barriers to entry in non-farm activities? What has been the impact of restructuring on the relative importance of 'push' and 'pull' factors for different strata of rural households?

A fourth issue raises questions about the role of small rural towns and infrastructural improvements in the development of the non-farm sector. Do they provide a stimulus to the growth of non-farm activities, or a base for better-endowed actors from outside the rural areas to out-compete rural non-farm enterprises?

The study that follows will address these issues as they relate to the context of the Nigerian savanna. Before proceeding to the actual case study, however, it is important to contextualize these issues with regard to the historical trends and theoretical concerns of the non-farm sector in rural northern Nigeria.

Historical perspectives: Non-farm activities and the rural economy in the Nigerian savanna

Contrary to the conventional image of rural Africa, non-farm activities have always played a significant role in the rural economy of the northern Nigerian savanna. While ecological factors have played a central role in this process, the interaction of cultural and political factors with the changing economic and policy context of the 20th century have tended, on the whole, to reinforce the economic importance of the non-farm sector. The savanna area of northern Nigeria is inhabited by the Hausa-Fulani (conventionally referred to simply as Hausa), who are predominantly Muslim. The influence of Islamic inheritance practices, the pre-colonial state system, and the development of commercial food crop agriculture since the beginning of the colonial period have combined to make access to land and labour more vulnerable to commercialization. This has tended to increase the importance of non-farm incomes, particularly among poor farmers. However, the shifting policy context of the colonial, independence and structural adjustment eras has produced significant fluctuations in the importance of non-farm activities relative to agriculture, particularly among wealthy farming households.

In the Nigerian savanna, a long history of urbanization and long-distance trade, which predates the colonial era by centuries, has contributed to the development of a wide range of non-farm activities. Both the manufacturing and trading activities associated with the prominence of such urban centres as Kano and Katsina involved extensive participation of rural artisans and traders. In particular, the central role of the Hausa in the kola, grain and livestock trades has resulted in a long history of circulation of rural inhabitants throughout the north of Nigeria, and south along the major trade routes as far as Lagos (Lovejoy 1980; Baier 1980; Cohen 1969; Hill 1977; Watts 1983). Rural inhabitants also played a central role in the spinning, weaving and dyeing of cotton cloth, a major industry and important export of the pre-colonial Hausa states of the central savanna. In addition, rural dwellers were involved in a range of local crafts such as blacksmithing, pottery, building, mat making, and other activities oriented toward the production of items for household and agricultural uses.

A wide range of studies point to a collapse of economic opportunities in the rural non-farm sector in the early years of colonialism, a period characterized by policy measures to promote the expansion of commercial grain production and export agriculture (Hill 1977; Bello 1982; Watts 1983). The early colonial period, which in northern Nigeria dates from the beginning of the twentieth century, witnessed the destruction of local crafts, owing to competition from imports and the deliberate suppression of certain activities by the colonial authorities, notably indigenous sugar and cloth production. These activities were felt to interfere with the production of varieties of sugar cane and cotton more suited to colonial industrial uses.

A countervailing trend that also dates from the colonial period involves the long-term shift of women's income generation toward non-agricultural activities. From the 1930s, there has been a rapid spread of the Islamic practice of wife seclusion into the rural areas. This has resulted in the near-total withdrawal of Muslim women from farming activities. Female participation in agriculture has been further limited by the ongoing conversion to Islam of many non-Muslim Hausa (Jackson 1985; Meagher 2000).

Trends toward a declining role of non-farm incomes among Hausa males appear to have been reversed by the policy environment of the Nigerian Oil Boom, which dates from the early 1970s. Evidence indicates a shift in favour of non-farm incomes, in the context of urban-biased development policies, discouraging terms of trade in agriculture, the pressures of agricultural commercialization, and rapacious policies of land acquisition for agricultural development schemes, state farms, private commercial agriculture and construction of educational and other institutions (Beckman 1987; Iliya & Swindell 1997). The result was an increase in landlessness or inadequate holdings, and high levels of rural-urban migration.

According to Jackson (1985), the economic and policy environment of the 1970s also encouraged a further shift of the activities of rural Hausa women in favour of the non-farm sector. Agricultural development programmes and large-scale irrigation schemes tended to further erode women's already restricted access to agricultural resources, while simultaneously expanding the profitability of women's non-farm activities. This tended to accentuate women's emphasis on non-farm sources of income.

It should be noted that the evidence regarding declining terms of trade in agriculture during the 1970s is mixed. Clough & Williams (1987), and Beckman (1987) argue that rapid urbanization, accelerating food price inflation and expanding markets for grain smuggling into Niger created expanding opportunities in the grain-based agriculture of the Nigerian savanna. This was, however, accompanied by the collapse of groundnut production, northern Nigeria's major export crop, and a dramatic expansion in the opportunities for non-farm incomes in the context of the Nigerian Oil

Boom. Furthermore, the capacity to benefit from opportunities in commercial grain production was determined by access to labour, modern inputs, and high value urban and cross-border markets - advantages biased heavily in favour of wealthy rural households, particularly in the context of the inflationary pressures of the Oil Boom (Meagher & Ogunwale 1994). Despite the development of profitable opportunities in commercial grain production, expanding opportunities in the non-farm sector appear to have been more attractive, since evidence suggests that, at least in larger villages and peri-urban areas, the reliance on non-farm incomes was highest among wealthy households during this period (Matlon 1977; Iliya & Swindell 1997).

The onset of economic crisis in the early 1980s brought about a contraction in both agricultural and non-farm opportunities. This appears to have provoked a rising share of non-farm incomes, in the context of a decline in overall income-generating options (Berry 1993a; Iliya & Swindell 1997). Following the imposition of Nigeria's Structural Adjustment Programme in 1986, the available evidence suggests that the income strategies of wealthier farmers shifted back in favour of agriculture. This is partly due to the fact that Nigeria's Structural Adjustment Programme, while containing many of the standard measures such as devaluation, trade and price liberalization, elimination of agricultural marketing boards, and elimination or reduction of a range of subsidies, also involved a range of distinctly illiberal measures which ran counter to the free-market logic of structural adjustment. These included distinctly pro-agricultural policies such as the imposition of bans on imports of rice, maize, wheat and barley, and the maintenance (despite attempts at reduction) of high subsidies on fertilizer (the most critical input for grain production in the savanna), and petrol (vital for trading grain to urban and border markets). Thus, in the face of a contraction of the urban economy under structural adjustment, the overall profitability of grain agriculture was initially increased by a combination of grain import bans, input subsidies, the creation of incentives for local sourcing of agro-industrial crops, and the stimulating effect of liberalization and devaluation on the cross-border grain trade with Niger (Andrae & Beckman 1987; Meagher & Ogunwale 1994). This created a situation of rising grain prices and expanding markets, in the context of more moderate rises in the cost of subsidized inputs (for those who could get them).

Unfortunately, small- and medium-scale farming households once again found themselves caught on the wrong side of the terms of trade. The high level of food deficit households in the Nigerian savanna, ranging between 10 and 20% of households even in good years, lost rather than benefited from rising grain prices (Matlon 1977; Meagher 1994). Moreover, the vast majority of farming households lacked access to significant quantities of subsidized fertilizer, leaving them at the mercy of fertilizer distributed via the open market. Even among grain surplus producers, rising grain prices were unable to keep pace with the increase in the open market price of fertilizer, except among farmers who had the resources and connections to gain access to large quantities of subsidised inputs, or to high-value urban or cross-border crop markets (Meagher & Mustapha 1997).

Women were also differentially affected by structural adjustment. Despite the constraints of seclusion, better-off women could fund access to land, labour and inputs in order to seize new opportunities in agriculture. They were also better placed to benefit from state and NGO initiatives to encourage female participation in agriculture (Lennihan 1994; Meagher 2000). Women from poorer households, however, lacked the capital to take up agricultural opportunities, and were also less able to sustain their non-farm activities in the face of the inflationary pressures of adjustment. The result was that the majority of women were forced in increasing numbers into a limited range of low-income non-farm activities (Meagher & Mustapha 1997).

These shifting historical trends raise questions about the role of the non-farm sector in northern Nigerian rural development, as well as its impact on rural social inequality. Does a shift of economic strategies in favour of non-farm incomes reflect a decline in the agricultural sector, or an increase in opportunities for income generation and accumulation among rural dwellers? Are these shifts in economic strategy governed largely by policy, or by longer-term structural and ecological factors within the rural economy? Do some strata of rural society benefit more from access to non-farm activities than others? What follows is a consideration of the northern

Nigerian theoretical debates generated by these issues, with a focus on the major shifts in theoretical concerns between the developmentalist era of the 1970s, and the era of crisis and structural adjustment, which in Nigeria dates from the early 1980s.

Theoretical perspectives of the 1960s and 1970s: Agricultural development and rural inequality

The agricultural economy of the Nigerian savanna was studied extensively from the late 1960s, owing in large part to the activities of the Institute of Agricultural Research, founded in Zaria in the early 1960s. While the primary focus of this research was agricultural, non-farm activities were recognized as significant components of rural incomes in northern Nigeria by the late 1960s and early 1970s. In two separate studies carried out in villages around Zaria and in south-western Kano State, 'off-farm' sources were found to account for roughly one-quarter of total household income, and 55% of cash income (Norman 1973a; Matlon 1977). In both cases, it was explicitly recognized that these figures under-represented the actual share of non-farm incomes, owing to the omission of data on women's incomes, which are almost exclusively non-agricultural (Matlon 1979; Norman et al. 1982).

In these early studies, linkages with the urban economy were regarded as a central determinant of the types of non-farm activities available, and of their share in the incomes of high-income households. In relatively remote villages, traditional activities dominated the non-farm sector, and non-farm earnings were lower, owing to weak markets and the narrow range of non-farm opportunities (Norman et al. 1982; Simmons 1975). Matlon (1977) noted that the lower share of non-farm incomes in remote villages was particularly marked in the case of wealthy households, who lacked access to the lucrative opportunities available in larger, more commercialized villages. In villages closer to urban centres, traditional crafts and services were undermined by competition from 'modern' substitutes, and a range of modern non-farm activities arose in the context of greater access to public and private sector employment as well as access to modern technology and inputs. In the long term, it was felt that increasing population pressure on land, combined with the low level of indigenous agricultural technology, would tend to increase the importance of non-farm incomes in total household incomes, unless efforts were made to increase the levels of agricultural technology through the introduction of improved inputs (Norman 1973a; Matlon 1979).

The 1970s and early 1980s represented a period of intense academic activity on issues relating to northern Nigerian agriculture, not only within agricultural disciplines, but from the perspectives of such disciplines as sociology, and political science. This plethora of academic activity generated a heated debate concerning the impact of agricultural modernization and commercialization on northern Nigerian rural society. Critical differences in perspective arose concerning the impact of non-farm activities on agriculture and on rural differentiation. On one side were those who argued that non-farm activities were essentially complementary with agricultural production, and dampened rural differentiation (Hill 1972; Clough & Williams 1987; Norman 1973a; Mortimore 1989). It was felt that the non-farm sector absorbed surplus labour, particularly in the off-season, among marginal farmers, and in times of poor rainfall, as well as contributing resources for agricultural intensification. Agricultural wage labour, which was regarded as a component of 'off-farm' income, was not seen to pose any threat to the persistence of peasant farming, since the low cash resources of labour-hiring farmers, and the own-farm demands of agricultural labourers, restricted the development of wage labour markets (Norman 1973a; Williams 1988).

On the other side of the debate, it was argued that non-farm incomes tended to widen income disparities, undermine peasant agriculture and reinforce rural differentiation (Matlon 1977; Beckman 1987; Watts 1983). Matlon's (1977) data on rural Kano indicated that economic barriers to entry tended to exclude low-income households from the more lucrative non-farm activities, restricting them to a range of low-income service activities. Moreover, data from villages around Zaria indicated that participation in non-farm activities, particularly agricultural wage labour, was found to undermine agricultural production among poorer households by diverting their efforts from agriculture, especially during the peak farming season. This was seen to reinforce the dependence of such households on non-farm activities (Lennihan 1987; see also Berry 1993a on southern Nigeria). In rural Kano, Matlon (1979) found that during the peak agricultural season, low-income males spent 22% of their time in non-farm activities, compared to only 5% among males from wealthy households.

Increasing awareness of the importance of women's incomes added a gender dimension to debates about the impact of non-farm incomes on rural inequality. Although the majority of Hausa women were largely excluded from agriculture by the rules of female seclusion, studies conducted during the course of the 1970s revealed a surprising degree of economic activity among secluded women (Simmons 1975; Hill 1969; Jackson 1985). Variations in the nature of female seclusion permitted limited female participation in agriculture, particularly among very poor households, post-menopausal women, women living outside nucleated rural settlements, and the non-Muslim Hausa (Meagher 2000; Imam 1993). Women also played an important role in the raising of small stock, such as sheep and goats, but this was largely a means of savings rather than income generation (Simmons 1975). Far more significant were a range of non-agricultural activities, based largely on crop and food processing, and a more limited participation in small-scale trade and local crafts. Access to inputs and circulation of goods was carried out through the agency of husbands, children or fostered children. In a study of over 400 women in three Zaria villages, Simmons (1975) found that at the time of interview, 95% of adult women were working in some form of income earning activity, 90% of them being involved in some form of food processing.

There was some disagreement as to the importance of women's incomes in overall household income, and their impact on rural income inequality. Hill (1977), Matlon (1978), and Norman et al. (1982) claimed that the economic role of women mitigated against the forces of differentiation. Matlon noted an inverse relationship between levels of female involvement in income-generating activities and the overall income status of households. He concluded that women from poorer households increased their levels of employment to compensate for inadequate male incomes. Watts (1983), on the other hand, argued that the withdrawal of female labour from farm work as a result of seclusion aggravated the serious labour constraint of poor households, a constraint that was unlikely to be compensated for by the limited incomes women were able to generate from within the confines of seclusion. Moreover, women's financial assistance to their husbands was normally made in the form of short-term credit, for which full repayment was expected. The economic role of women was therefore seen to reinforce rural income inequality and to accelerate the dependence of poorer households on non-farm sources of income.

Assessments of the long-term potential of non-farm incomes in the rural development process were less neatly polarized than debates about the role of non-farm incomes in rural inequality. Norman (1973a) maintained that non-farm activities had a potential for labour absorption and poverty alleviation, but had little long-term potential for raising rural incomes. Others argued that non-farm incomes provided important opportunities for income support for the poor and accumulation for the wealthy, but felt that the existing technical and social framework of the rural economy would prevent any dramatic increases in rural inequality (Clough & Williams 1987; Matlon 1979; Williams 1988). A third position held that non-farm incomes contributed to processes that undermine peasant agriculture (Beckman 1987; Wallace 1978), and, in the extreme formulation, would contribute to the elimination of the peasantry (Watts 1983). Common to all of these positions was a perception that the engine of rural growth lay in agriculture. Non-farm incomes were perceived as developmental only insofar as they contributed to increasing the ability of households to invest in agriculture, and were 'anti-developmental' to the extent that they drew labour or other resources out of agriculture.

Perspectives of the 1980s and 1990s:
The role of ecology, policy and economic restructuring

By the 1980s, there was a growing recognition in the northern Nigerian literature that factors other than agricultural technology, population pressure on land and the gender division of labour affected the role of non-farm activities in rural income-generation. Increasing concerns about the environmental sustainability of African agriculture, and the dramatic impact of economic crisis and structural adjustment drew attention to the role of ecology, policy, and household livelihood strategies in determining the economic importance of the non-farm sector. While previous studies showed an awareness of the relationship between ecological factors and activity patterns, the concern with desertification and sustainability emerged as central policy issue during the late 1970s and early 1980s, largely as a result of the severe 1972-74 Sahellian drought, and subsequent evidence of declining rainfall patterns since the early 1970s. The growing economic crisis from the early 1980s and the imposition of structural adjustment, have served to intensify the policy concern with issues of adaptation and sustainability of rural livelihoods. As a result, the focus of research on non-farm activities has shifted from trajectories of sectoral change, to more flexible processes of adaptation to variations in climatic and economic conditions.

From the perspective of ecology, Mortimore (1989) focused on the ways in which non-farm incomes contribute to the sustainability of agriculture in a fragile agricultural environment. He argued that non-farm incomes, earned largely through patterns of cyclical migration, represent a form of adaptation to an agricultural environment characterized by uncertain rainfall and cycles of drought. Meteorological evidence has shown declining rainfall levels since the early 1970s in the sahel savanna of the far north of Nigeria, forcing an increased dependence on non-farm sources of income (Mortimore 1989; Mustapha & Meagher 1992). In the guinea savanna immediately to the south, there is no evidence of a decline in annual rainfall levels, but the area is troubled by an increasing unreliability in rainfall patterns, which has a negative effect on crop yields. Within this context, a shift in favour of non-farm incomes reflects a stabilizing force within the rural economy.

An alternative perspective has emphasized the role of policy and economic change in determining trends in the relationship between agricultural and non-farm incomes. Lubeck (1987) for example challenged the notion that shifts between agricultural and non-farm incomes represent timeless adaptive processes unaffected by economic and social constraints created by the prevailing policy environment. He pointed out that, owing to the very limited penetration of Western education and technical skills in the rural areas of the Islamic north, the urban income-generating options of the majority of Hausa migrants are concentrated in a narrow range of marginal service activities (see also Meagher 1997; Meagher & Yunusa 1996). The coincidence of the inflationary pressures of the Nigerian Oil Boom and subsequent economic crisis with a sustained period of declining rainfall and drought put severe pressure on the incomes from these marginal urban activities. These tensions erupted in a series of violent riots in the early 1980s and again in the 1990s, which have increasingly been targeted at the more technically skilled and economically successful Igbo migrants from south-eastern Nigeria. Work by Berry (1993b) and Guyer & Idowu (1991) on south-western Nigeria also suggests that the uncertainty and agricultural instability created by economic crisis and adjustment tends to increase the dependence of rural households on non-farm incomes, often with undesirable consequences for local ecological management practices and women's economic burdens within the household.

Long-term perspectives on the role of policy in determining the relationship of farm to non-farm incomes reveal an increasingly complex picture. Recent studies by Meagher & Mustapha (1997) and Iliya & Swindell (1997) indicate that movements between agricultural and non-farm incomes in northern Nigeria are neither recent nor uni-directional, nor do such shifts tend to be consistent across socio-economic strata. Both studies argue that dependence on non-farm incomes rose during the Oil Boom years of the 1970s, and began to decline from the early 1980s owing largely to the contraction of urban non-farm opportunities and rising prices of agricultural commodities. Iliya & Swindell speak of a process of 're-agrarianization' since the imposition of structural adjustment – a trend influenced less by agricultural liberalization than by the more illiberal measures of Nigeria's structural adjustment programme, including the bans on grain imports and the maintenance of subsidies on officially distributed fertilizer.

However, both studies argue that the overall shift in favour of agricultural incomes masks divergent tendencies among different strata of the rural population. Wealthy households show a marked decline in the share of non-farm incomes, owing to the rising profitability of grain and irrigated crop production since the mid-1980s. Poor households show the reverse tendency – a marked rise in the share of non-farm incomes – owing to a lack of resources necessary to shift their livelihood strategies back in favour of agriculture in the context of rapid inflation in land, labour and input prices, combined with the rising cost of living. Households in the middle group show mixed tendencies. In both studies, attention is drawn to the superior capacity of wealthy households to maintain access to land, labour and capital in the face of rapid changes in economic and policy conditions. Iliya & Swindell (1997), who focus largely on peri-urban areas, emphasize the critical role of political patronage and wealth accumulated through remittances from salaried jobs. Meagher & Mustapha (1977), who consider villages located deeper in the rural areas, focus on the importance of wealth accumulated through rural activities, primarily trade and agriculture, as well as control of and investment in a range of rural social networks.

The impact of structural adjustment on economic relations within rural households has also received some attention in the literature on northern Nigeria. The central focus relates to the impact of adjustment on women's non-farm activities, pressures toward increased economic responsibilities within the household, and the extent to which women are able to seize increased opportunities in agriculture. Meagher & Mustapha (1997) cite evidence of squeezed profits in the bulk of women's non-farm activities, owing to rising input costs and weakening markets. Lennihan (1994) and Meagher (2000) have noted a limited trend toward 're-agrarianization' among wealthier Hausa women in response to a range of state incentives and the rising profitability of commercial agriculture. The limitations of female seclusion tend to restrict this option to wealthy women, owing to the necessity of farming largely through hired labour. Imam (1993) and Meagher (2000) consider the ways in which the continued practice of seclusion – and the ideological framework of male household provisioning which supports it – masks a shift of the pressures of household provisioning onto women, particularly those from poorer households.

Quantitative evidence on trends in non-farm income shares, 1972-1993

A final issue to draw out from the literature is what available quantitative data can tell us about long-term trends in the importance of non-farm incomes. Detailed quantitative data for the Nigerian guinea savanna exist from the late 1960s. As earlier mentioned, non-farm incomes in two grain surplus areas of the savanna were found to account for 24% of total household incomes in the 1966/7 agricultural year (Norman 1973b), and 28% of household incomes in 1974/5 (Matlon 1979).[1] While the data appear to invite an interpretation of rising non-farm income shares, it should be noted that Matlon's 1974/5 data include livestock income under the non-farm category, while Norman's earlier studies do not. Taking account of livestock incomes obliterates the apparent rise in non-farm income shares.

Matlon's data also indicates that non-farm incomes represented an average of 55% of household cash incomes in the mid-1970s. Directly comparable studies were conducted some fifteen years later in the most commercialized of the villages studied by Matlon. These studies indicate that non-farm incomes accounted for an average of 60% of total cash incomes in the 1989/90 agricultural year, and 53% of total cash incomes in the 1992/3 agricultural year (Meagher 1991; Meagher & Ogunwale 1994) (see Table 2.1). Time-series data on non-farm shares of total household incomes in cash and kind were not available. It should be noted that, like Norman's and

---

[1] The data invite comparison, given that in both studies, it includes agricultural wage labour and excludes women's income, as well as representing in both cases an average of three villages, ranging from the relatively isolated to the highly commercialized or peri-urban.

Matlon's original data, the figures from the later studies include agricultural wage labour in non-farm incomes, but do not include women's incomes, which are predominantly non-farm. This increases the comparability of the data across time, but understates by as much as 10-15% the actual share of non-farm incomes in household cash incomes.

Table 2.1
Share of non-farm activities in total cash income in Rogo Village, Nigeria 1974/5-1992/3 (%)

Farming category	1974/5*	1989/90**	1992/3***
Small-scale	53.2	60.4	67.0
Medium-scale	49.0	67.7	57.4
Large-scale	84.4	58.3	46.6
Average	55.7	59.7	53.0

*   Matlon (1977). Small-scale farmers represent the first two quintiles of Matlon's sample, Medium-scale the third and fourth quintiles, and large-scale the fifth quintile. Figures do not include women's incomes. Income from livestock is classified as non-farm.

**   Meagher (1991). Figures do not include women's income, or incomes from livestock or gifts.

*** Meagher & Ogunwale 1994. Figures do not include women's incomes or incomes from livestock or gifts.

Source: Meagher & Mustapha 1997.

Despite the limitations of the data, they can still be used to convey a rough picture of trends in non-farm incomes shares. Given the sparseness of the data, however, the authoritativeness of these trends should not be over-stated. The available data indicate that, at least as regards cash incomes, non-farm income shares have been characterized by fluctuations around a mean rather than by a clear rising trend. In the northern guinea savanna, non-farm income shares have fluctuated around a mean of approximately 56%. This is consistent with the historical analyses presented above, which point to fluctuations in the importance of the non-farm sector depending on movements in agricultural terms of trade and changes in government policy.

However, more interesting trends are revealed in the disaggregated data on non-farm income shares of different socio-economic strata. The disaggregated data indicate a clear upward trend in non-farm income shares among small-scale farmers, and a distinct downward trend in non-farm income shares among large-scale farmers. The medium-scale group show a fluctuating trend. It is worth noting that these trends would have been slightly accentuated by the inclusion of women's incomes, given their heavily non-farm composition and quantitative evidence of their inverse relationship to household income levels (Matlon 1978).

An analysis of the periods of data collection adds to the story. The mid-1970s corresponds to the Oil Boom period, when non-farm opportunities were rising, and terms of trade in northern Nigerian agriculture were poor.[2] The end of the 1980s corresponds to a period when terms of trade in commercial grain production were at their peak, and 1991/2 corresponds to the year in which fertilizer prices began to rise dramatically and terms of trade in commercial grain production began to decline. Thus, the data corroborates earlier evidence that, where non-farm opportunities are expanding, as during the Oil Boom, better-off households tend to diversify more. Conversely, where agricultural opportunities are expanding, the poor, who lack the land, labour or capital to exploit them, show higher levels of diversification than the wealthy.

It must be kept in mind that the data relate to cash incomes, and tell us nothing about changes in the relationship of cash incomes to total household incomes in cash and kind. While the rapid process of commercialization in the area suggests that the share of cash incomes in total incomes must be rising, which would tend to increase the share of non-farm incomes in total household incomes, there is no information on the rate of increase, or on differential trends in these rates among different strata of farming households. If there has been a rapid increase in dependence on cash incomes over the past thirty years, which seems probable, then average non-farm income shares could actually be rising relative to total household incomes, though it

---

[2]   Northern Nigeria's groundnut-based export agriculture had just collapsed, and terms of trade were only beginning to shift in favour of commercial grain production.

is clear that such a trend would largely be propelled by the poorer socio-economic strata.

The literature reviewed above has shown that the non-farm sector has a long and complex history in northern Nigeria. Whether the analysis focuses on ecology, state policy or relations within the household, a critical point that emerges is that the changing role of the non-farm sector in rural livelihoods is neither a unilineal nor a socially harmonious process. Over the past century, changes in the economic, social and policy context have triggered significant fluctuations in the importance of the non-farm sector, rather than a secular rise in non-farm dependence. Moreover, the direction of change has varied between men and women, as well as between poor and wealthy rural households. Since the 1980s, the apparent increase in the economic role of the non-farm sector has been accompanied by an intensification of tensions over access to resources and opportunities, at the level of the household, the community, and the wider society. The case study that follows will consider how the changing relationship between the agricultural and non-farm sectors, and the social tensions generated in the process, have played themselves out in the village of Nasarawan Doya in the economic and policy context of the late 1990s.

3

Methodology

Coming to grips with the wide range of factors that influence the role of the non-farm sector in the rural economy of northern Nigeria is a complex endeavour. As the preceding literature review has indicated, one is not confronting a unilineal developmental or degenerative process, but a labyrinth of historical, cultural, economic and policy factors which have produced oscillating terms of trade between agricultural and non-farm activities, with differing consequences for men and women, and for various strata of the rural population. Attempting to reflect these complexities within the context of a single study has posed a powerful methodological challenge.

The aim of the study was to investigate the role of the non-farm economy in a manner which would capture both the broad economic trends, and the differentiating or contextual features of class, gender, ethnicity, community, ecology and policy change which give social and historical depth to the economic data. This required the collection of detailed quantitative economic data on households as well as non-farm enterprises, while maintaining a sensitivity to the myriad structural, cultural and historical factors which have shaped trends in the non-farm economy. The difficulties en-

42

Map indicating the study location

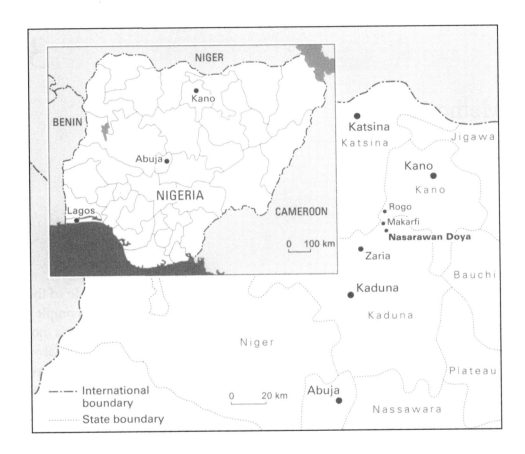

countered in accomplishing this task are reflected in the complicated structure of samples, the wide-ranging categories of data collection, and the sometimes convoluted structure of a study attempting to knit together a comprehensive narrative from an astonishing range and diversity of material.

What follows here represents an attempt to orient the reader before launching into the study itself. The orientation begins with a description of the setting of the study, which involves the presentation of the village of Nasarawan Doya as a geographical, historical and social entity. This is followed by an explanation of the methodology of the study, involving a definition of key concepts and a justification of the methods used. Finally, some of the central methodological problems encountered in the course of the research and subsequent analysis are highlighted, with a view to identifying the limitations of the data presented.

Nasarawan Doya: A village and a setting

The village of Nasarawan Doya is located in northern Kaduna State, in the grain-based agricultural surplus region of northern Nigeria known as the northern guinea savanna. The region is characterized by a relatively short and unreliable rainy season, extending from April to September, and a long dry season. Average annual rainfall in the area around Nasarawan Doya is approximately 900 mm. Nasarawan Doya enjoys fairly good access to a range of rural and urban market centres. Just under 10 kilometres of semi-motorable dirt road separate Nasarawan Doya from the federally maintained highway linking the urban centres of Kano and Kaduna, both of which lie over 100 km from the village in opposite directions. Zaria, the closest urban centre and traditional political capital of the area, is 35 km from Nasarawan Doya. 13 km in the opposite direction lies the rural market town of Makarfi, the site of a major rural bulking market for agricultural crops, and the headquarters of the Local Government Area.

A 1996 assessment registered the population of Nasarawan Doya as 12,625 inhabitants. The bulk of the population are Hausa-Fulani, a Muslim

Hausa-speaking group composed of Islamized Hausa and settled Fulani peoples. In the outlying hamlets are also small pockets of Christian Hausa, and semi-settled and nomadic Fulani, which constitute collectively less than 10 percent of the total village population. There are also a couple of households from other regions of Nigeria – largely of Igbo and Yoruba origins – as well as a handful of single young men from various parts of northern and southern Nigeria, all of whom have come to Nasarawan Doya to pursue a range of non-farm activities.

Farming, for consumption and sale, is the major source of livelihood in the village. The area around the village is suited to both upland farming (*tudu*) and small-scale river-bottom irrigated farming (*fadama*), which per-mits extensive dry season agriculture. The staple crops grown in the area are sorghum and maize, which are also important cash crops. The other major cash crops of the area are sugar cane, peppers, rice, groundnuts, cowpeas, and soyabeans. Farming is predominantly a male activity in Nasarawan Doya, owing to the practice of a strict form of female seclusion among the Muslim Hausa-Fulani majority. Among Hausa-Fulani women, direct parti-cipation in farming can only be undertaken via household or hired labour, or by women past child-bearing age. Female seclusion is not practised among the Christian Hausa and pastoral Fulani, and Christian Hausa women in particular are active in farming.

Livestock production is also widely practised, predominantly involving cattle, sheep, goats and chickens. Unusually for this part of rural northern Nigeria, roughly one third of the households also own at least one horse, which is used to operate sugar cane crushing machines. While livestock production plays a central role in the livelihoods of the pastoral Fulani in the outlying hamlets, it is of fairly minor overall importance as a source of income generation in the village. The economic role of non-farm activities is much more significant. A wide range of non-farm activities are also prac-tised by the inhabitants, ranging from agricultural wage labour, traditional crafts and petty trade, to large-scale crop trading, local sugar production, modern crafts and a limited number of salaried positions in nearby rural and urban centres.

Nasarawan Doya is said to have been founded in the late 18th century by migrants from Katsina, Kano, Gobir and Niger. It is composed of four wards, three of which are clustered in the town centre, while the remaining ward encompasses a range of scattered hamlets on the outskirts of the main centre. The village has a weekly market, which was established about 100 years ago. The market is held on Fridays, and attracts traders and consumers from the surrounding villages, from the rural town of Makarfi, as well as from the urban centres of Zaria and Kano. The market is particularly known as a source of sorghum and maize. The village also has 24 local shops, specializing in a range of manufactured household consumer goods (known locally as 'provisions') and used clothing, as well as two chemists.

Nasarawan Doya has a range of public facilities, but most of them are barely operational. The village primary school, established in 1970, has little in the way of teaching materials, and few students. The village also has a dispensary, established in 1971, and a clinic, established in 1978. The dispensary has had no staff and no medicine for years, and during the course of the research was converted into a makeshift police station. The clinic is staffed with one health officer, one nurse and some local health workers, but has no medicine. A private clinic, opened in 1996 in two rented rooms in the village, remained closed throughout 1997 owing to an insufficient number of patients. In 1997, the village was allocated a police officer following serious incidents of armed robbery.

Public utilities are similarly weak. Water is obtained largely through local wells, which tend to dry up during the dry season, causing serious water shortage. A borehole was constructed in 1983, but broke down in 1996, and was not repaired during the entire period of the research. There is no electricity, though the village has a telephone. The dirt road is maintained only by communal efforts, and is only laboriously navigable during the rainy season. Nonetheless, transport links between the village and surrounding regional and urban centres are fairly good, owing to the services of a commercial vehicle, which runs passenger services in and out of the village several times per day. There are only four other motor vehicles in the village, including the private car belonging to the village head, though motorcycles and bicycles abound.

Research methodology

Fieldwork for this study was conducted between July 1996 and June 1997. The timing of the research was chosen to cover the three major seasons of non-farm activity in the area: the 'wet' season (*damina*), the 'dry' or 'harvest' season (*rani*) and the 'hot' (*bazara*) season,[1] and to permit economic monitoring of both agricultural and non-farm activities at the end of each of these seasons in September, January and May.

In an effort to reflect the interrelation of the agricultural and non-farm sectors, two types of samples were taken from the village: a household sample and a non-farm enterprise sample. The aim was to capture in sufficient detail both the role of non-farm activities in household livelihood strategies, and the enterprise-level dynamics of a wider range of non-farm activities, including several strategic enterprises carried out by migrants who were not members of local households.

The value of the data collected from the two samples rests heavily on appropriate definitions of the two key concepts used to define them: the concepts of 'household' and 'non-farm sector'. Both of these concepts have a long and contentious history in African social science literature. For the purposes of this study, definitions were chosen to reflect as closely as

---

[1] The local terminology, involving three distinct seasons, was taken as the basis of the seasonal divisions used in the study, despite its sometimes awkward interaction with English seasonal terminology used in the savanna. While the wet season posed no problems, being marked by the start and cessation of the rains, the conventional usage of the term 'dry season' tends to blur together two distinct seasons as distinguished by local terminology and occupational behaviour. The first half of the dry season (*rani*) is a largely cold season which last from the cessation of the rains in September to the end of the cold period in January. Although this is the season most strongly associated with non-agricultural activities, it is also heavily occupied with agricultural activities relating to the harvest, with the traditional staple, sorghum, along with key varieties of beans, being harvested in November and December. The second half of the dry season (*bazara*) is a hot and humid period which lasts from February until the rains begin in April/May. In this study, I have used the term 'dry season' (and occasionally 'harvest season', or 'harmattan') to refer only to the dry, dusty, cold season which covers the first half of the non-rainy period. The term 'hot season' has been used to refer to the second half of the non-rainy period.

possible the dynamics of social organization and economic change in rural Hausa society.

The issue of the 'non-farm sector' concept has already been addressed above. In studies of rural northern Nigeria, the concept of households has proven equally contentious. 'Households' were defined as units of production rather than as units of consumption or co-habitation. While this departs from the definition used by Norman (1973a), it conforms better to Hausa patterns of agricultural organization, in which a household may be defined as a unit of production comprising male relatives who farm jointly, together with their wives, children and other dependents (Hill 1972). Owing to the individualizing pressures of agricultural commercialization, few households still farm in joint production units of related adult males, traditionally known as *gandu*. Such units are now predominantly found among wealthy households, or among the christian and pagan Hausa (known as the *Maguzawa*). Among low- and middle-income households, the male heads frequently farm alone in household units which resemble a nuclear family (*iyali*).

The household sample used in the study involved a systematic random sample of 100 farming households, selected from the village tax list. A structured questionnaire was administered to household heads only, focusing on general household characteristics, agricultural (farming and livestock) and non-farm activities within the household, levels of agricultural production, occupational aspirations and assessments of the prospects of agriculture and non-farm activities under current economic conditions.

In order to collect more detailed information on the activities, incomes and attitudes of other household members, a sub-sample of 40 households was randomly selected from the main sample. Questionnaires were administered to all economically active members of the household, including wives and male and female dependents. This involved a three-phased monitoring of each economically active member, carried out at the end of each of the three main agricultural seasons (rainy, harvest and dry), focusing on income in cash and kind from all economic activities, as well as income from gifts.

On the basis of an independent survey of all non-farm activities in the village, an additional sample of 50 non-farm enterprises was selected. Activities were divided into occupational categories, and a stratified purposive sample was selected to represent large and small-scale operators in each of the various categories. A questionnaire was administered to this group, focusing on enterprise characteristics, and the impact of current economic conditions on income levels, as well as on access to capital, inputs and labour. In the household as well as the enterprise samples, the questionnaire-based surveys were supplemented with indepth oral interviews with a range of respondents within as well as outside the samples.

In order to consider the role of economic inequality in developments in the non-farm sector, the various samples were stratified. In the household sample and sub-sample, stratification was based on access to agricultural labour. In the relatively commercialized and broadly land-surplus conditions of the Nigerian savanna, studies have indicated that the classification of households in terms of net labour purchases or sales is a more important indicator of socio-economic position than landholdings or income (Longhurst 1985; Mustapha 1990). Accordingly, households in the main sample and sub-sample were stratified according to a measurement of the household head's net sales or purchases of agricultural labour. Household heads who performed more agricultural labour than they used on the household farm were placed in the lower stratum, those who performed less than 10% of the labour used on the household farm were placed in the upper stratum, and those in between were placed in the middle stratum. In the household sample of 100 households, 51 belonged to the lower stratum, 42 belonged to the middle stratum, and 7 to the upper stratum.

In the case of the sample of non-farm enterprises, the different economic logic and composition of this group required a different basis of stratification from that used in the household sample. Unlike the household sample, the enterprise sample included migrants, some of whom did not farm but were among the most successful entrepreneurs in the village. Given that the majority of the enterprises investigated were owner-operated, and that the nature of the activity appeared a more critical measure of income generating potential than access to labour *per se*, capital rather than labour was chosen as the basis for stratification in the enterprise sample. The sample was stratified into two groups based on the amount of capital necessary to start up a given enterprise in 1997 prices. Due in part to the purposive nature of the sample selection, 50% of the sample was in the top category, and 50% in the bottom category, although this even distribution was not expressly intended in the design of the sample.

Given the relatively small size of the various samples, analysis of variation within the samples necessarily involves very small numbers with limited statistical significance. The objective of the statistical analysis is therefore not so much to prove, as to illustrate patterns of behaviour and of socio-economic relationships.

The more quantitative orientation used in the analysis of the various samples was supplemented by a range of qualitative techniques, largely case studies and historical interviews. Approximately fifteen individual case studies were collected, across generational, occupational and gender categories. These case studies focused on changes in non-agricultural activities over time, sources of non-farm capital, and the relationship between agricultural and non-agricultural activities in the organization of livelihood strategies. Five historical interviews were also conducted with old men and one old woman in the village who were deemed to be knowledgeable about changes in non-farm activity patterns at the village level. One of these village-level historical authorities was born around or before the turn of the century, and, sadly, died shortly before the conclusion of the fieldwork. The remaining three had clear memories that went back to the 1930s and 1940s, yielding useful insights into the impact of female seclusion and the penetration of modern non-farm activities into the village. The information gathered in these interviews was verified by cross-comparison among informants and reference to the abundant historical literature on rural northern Nigeria.

Methodological problems

Owing to difficulties with the timing and design of the study, and the fundamental problems of quantification in a rural African environment, a number of contentious issues arose in the process of data collection and analysis. The timing of the study confronted a problem of representativeness right from the very beginning, owing to the fact that it coincided with a severe fertilizer distribution crisis, which dramatically affected agricultural production, livelihood strategies and income levels in the area. However, the fertilizer-related pressures that arose between 1996 and 1997 represented an acute manifestation of a longer-term problem of northern Nigerian agriculture, rather than any departure from prevailing trends. The result was to dramatize rather than distort the major trends in the development and relationship of agricultural and non-agricultural activities. In the interest of a balanced assessment, however, economic behaviour directly attributable to the 1996-7 fertilizer crisis were identified as such.

A second difficulty arose in the context of conflicting aims between the sampling strategy and objectives of stratification. In the household sample, the definition of households as production units was deliberately chosen to represent the widest possible generational spread of household heads, from old compound heads to young men who had recently broken away from their father's production unit. The central aim was to represent the strategies and concerns of younger as well as older adult males, along with their households, so as to capture generational differences in skills, occupational identities and access to factors of agricultural production.

Unfortunately, an unintended effect of this procedure was to dampen evidence of socio-economic differentiation, which is obviously weaker where there is significant influence of life-cycle factors. Wealthy young heads just starting up independent households may have structural advantages which place them in the top socio-economic category, but are likely to score less well on such indicators as income, assets, or household size than much older and better established heads in the middle category, who have larger households and have had a much longer period within which to accumulate assets. Clearly, stratified averages of indicators of economic wealth do not distinguish between the capacity to accumulate, controlling for age, and the actual stage of accumulation a particular head has reached in terms of the head's – and the household's – life cycle.

A further problem arose in the context of the household sub-sample which involved 40 households selected randomly from the main household sample. While Norman argues that a sample of 40 is sufficiently represent-ative in the context of rural northern Nigeria, it was found that this is not necessarily the case if the sample is further stratified. In the household sub-sample, the upper stratum captured only two members (compared to 7 members in the main household sample), both of whom turned out to be particularly unrepresentative of their stratum. The first was a young man of 25, who was extremely well-off for his stage in life, but rated significantly lower on many indicators than older and better-established household heads in the middle stratum. The second was a very old man in his 70s, who used outside sources for most of the labour used on his farm largely because of age and infirmity rather than wealth. Owing to these difficulties, the house-hold sub-sample was stratified into two, rather than three socio-economic groups. The upper and middle strata of the main household sample were amalgamated into a single upper stratum in the sub-sample, while the lower stratum was defined in the same way in both samples.

In the process of data collection, difficulties were confronted in the quantification of a number of critical variables. These included age, levels of agricultural production and income, and profits from non-farm activities. Many of the respondents were either unable or unwilling to estimate their ages. Attempts to approximate ages accurately by locating the time of birth with relation to important local events proved more successful, but was so time consuming that it began to interfere with the successful completion of the questionnaires, and had to be abandoned. The ages, especially of some of the older respondents, therefore represent approximations in many cases.

In the case of agricultural production levels, problems arose, not in the area of quantification *per se*, but in the area of comparability and aggre-gation. Agricultural producers in this area can recall with a high degree of accuracy the quantities harvested and sold in the current, and also in the previous, agricultural year. However, answers are most accurate if given in local units, which frequently vary from crop to crop, and do not necessarily distinguish between shelled and unshelled produce, making conversion to standard measures a complex procedure.

Further problems arose in the valuation of these crops for the purposes of calculating agricultural and non-farm income shares. Here, the valuation of unmarketed crops posed problems owing to the fact that prices for a given crop vary considerably according to time and location of sale, quality and variety of the crop, and the economic pressure facing the seller. For the purposes of this study, it was decided to value unmarketed crops according the average price of the equivalent marketed crops within the household sample. The alternative of using local average annual prices was unsuitable, because producers from Nasarawan Doya market their crops in a wide range of village, bulking and urban markets, all of which have very different annual price ranges. Unmarketed sugar cane posed a particular problem owing to its use as a raw material for household sugar production enterprises. For this reason, no value was calculated for unmarketed sugar cane under the category of agricultural income, since it invariably reappeared in the form of income from local sugar production under the category of non-farm income.

Attempts to estimate weekly profits from non-farm activities were even more problematic. It became clear that operators define profits as what is left by the end of the week, although in many cases, a significant amount of what is earned is spent during the course of the week on various household needs. In order to circumvent this problem, it was necessary to focus data collection on turnover, which respondents were able to recall more accurately. Thus, calculations of total incomes are based on gross incomes, inclusive of production costs, in both agriculture and non-farm activities. Calculations of income shares for agricultural and non-farm incomes should therefore be treated as rough orders of magnitude, which were deemed adequate for the purposes of comparison and identification of trends, but do not represent actual disposable income.

4

The determinants of non-farm participation: Household inequality and agricultural restructuring

We will turn now to an analysis of the determinants of non-farm participation from the perspective of agriculture. Two levels of analysis are relevant here. The first concerns the nature of pressures or opportunities within agriculture, which may motivate a rise or a decline in non-farm participation. The second concerns the characteristics or 'assets' of rural households that influence their ability to gain access to adequate non-farm incomes (Gordon 1999; Reardon et al. 1998). These two dimensions have been dubbed 'push' and 'pull' factors, respectively. As the historical perspective on non-farm participation in the Nigerian savanna has shown, the central issue in analysing both the push and pull factors is that of rural inequality and its impact on livelihood options. For a comprehensive understanding of diversification strategies, what is called for is an analysis of the ways in which inequalities in access to land, labour and capital in agriculture influence both incentives to diversify and terms of entry into the non-farm sector.

A further issue to be factored into the analysis is the impact of ongoing changes in agriculture on the diversification process. In the context of the Nigerian savanna, this relates primarily to negative changes in the impact of structural adjustment policies on agricultural terms of trade since the beginning of the 1990s. The aim here is to challenge the tendency in some of the current non-farm literature to detach issues of access to non-farm incomes from the wider question of how processes of economic restructuring have influenced the viability of agricultural livelihoods. Structural adjustment policies are prescribed as a useful means of loosening up conditions of access to non-farm incomes, without ever considering the effect of these policies on the forces underlying diversification. The argument put forward here is that current trends in non-farm participation cannot be adequately understood unless the issue of access to non-farm incomes is examined in the context of the impact of economic restructuring on agricultural livelihoods.

The analysis that follows will examine the way in which rural inequality and changes in agricultural conditions have influenced patterns of diversification into the non-farm activities. It will begin with an analysis of the prominence of labour rather than land in the determination of agricultural inequalities in the Nigerian savanna. This will be used to structure an understanding of the differential impact of pressures on agricultural livelihoods ('push' factors) within the context of structural adjustment. The analysis will then turn to an examination of 'pull' factors, which are found to reinforce rather than moderate patterns of agriculturally-based economic inequality. Key determinants of access to non-farm incomes in the context of Nasarawan Doya are access to capital and household composition. By contrast with other regions, land and education are, for the moment, comparatively limited in their impact on non-farm income inequality among the current generation of household heads, but both are beginning to shape household inequalities via the incomes of rural youth.

The determinants of agricultural inequality

In terms of ethnicity, religion, primary occupation, and a range of other social variables, Nasarawan Doya represents a highly homogeneous population, as is typical of much of the grain surplus region of the savanna. The ethno-religious composition of the sample households was overwhelmingly Hausa, and overwhelmingly Muslim. The only minority ethnic grouping, constituting only 6%, were Fulani, all of whom were also Muslim. There was only one non-Muslim in the entire sample, a Christian Hausa household living in the outlying hamlets. Over 90% of the household heads were indigenes of Nasarawan Doya, and the remaining household heads came from villages in the vicinity, or from neighbouring states (Kano and Katsina) with ethnically and culturally similar populations. Owing to the influence of Islamic norms of social organization, all of the households in the sample were male-headed. While in exceptional circumstances, female-headed households do occur in this area, they are extremely rare. Female-headed households numbered under 1% of the village households at the time of study, and tend to be associated either with professional prostitution or widows/divorcees who are sufficiently wealthy to resist social and economic pressures to remarry or return to their natal household. The conventional association of female-headedness with poverty does not necessarily hold in this context.

Participation in agriculture was almost universal. All but one of the households engaged in wet season farming. The only non-farmer was a head whose land was frozen in a land dispute. In addition, more than three-quarters of the households engaged in dry season farming, and 85% kept some form of livestock. Both dry season farming and livestock keeping were slightly biased in favour of better-off households. Farming activities in the area are relatively commercialized, and the use of commercial inputs and hired labour is widespread. 98% of the households used chemical fertilizer, and 68% used at least some hired labour.[1] All in all, factors of ethnicity,

---

[1] By contrast, just under 20% of households owned ox-ploughs, while an additional 10% hired them, making roughly 30% of households using animal traction.

religion, participation in farming and the gender of the household head were not found to be central differentiating factors among village households.

Table 4.1
Rural inequality and average levels of wet season agricultural production and sales, 1995/6*

Stratum	Number	Average wet season harvest (100kg bags)	Average sales of wet season crops (100kg bags)
Upper	7	650	475
Middle	42	84	49
Lower	51	35	18
Sample Average	1000	99	63

* Occasional minor crops not harvested in units convertible to 100 kg bags were excluded from averages.
Source: Fieldwork 1996-97

In the context of this socially homogeneous population, there is significant economic differentiation. In the traditionally land-surplus conditions of the savanna, access to agricultural labour has functioned as the key determinant of economic inequality. Table 4.1 examines the pattern of economic stratification within the village. The upper stratum includes households who hire in more than 90% of the labour they use for farming. The lower stratum are those who perform more agricultural labour than they require on the household farm – that is, they do most or all of their own farming, and hire out their labour to other farmers as well. The middle stratum are those who perform between 10% and 100% of the agricultural labour they require. These strata are associated with significant differences in average levels of crop production and sales. While upper stratum farmers produced an average of 650 100kg bags of crops on their wet season farms in 1995/6, lower stratum farmers produced an average of only 35 bags. Similarly in the case of sales, upper stratum households sold more than 25 times the quantity marketed by lower stratum households.

Land: Equalizer or push factor?

In contrast to Asia and Latin America, as well as some other parts of Africa, land has not yet become a significant differentiating factor in most of the Nigerian savanna. Within the household sub-sample (which was stratified into only two groups because of smaller numbers), detailed investigation and measurement of land-holdings for all household members was under-taken.[2] Average household landholdings were found to amount to 3.45 hectares, which is more than adequate to support a household in this region. Variations in average land holdings between upper and lower-stratum households were fairly minor, at 3.79 ha. and 3.08 ha. respectively (Table 4.2), and there were no landless households. Although not captured in the sample, there are a few exceptionally large holdings within the village, reaching as much as 500 ha., but these are related to political rather than economic forms of access. Except in the few cases of political access, land holdings are only weakly associated with socio-economic status. Many of the largest holdings in the sample belonged to relatively poor households in the lower stratum, largely the more geographically and economically iso-lated residents of the outlying hamlets.

Although average land holdings are relatively similar at the household level, it is important to note that, at the individual level, average holdings of household heads are significantly less in the lower than in the upper stratum. This is compensated for largely by average holdings among male de-pendents and women in the lower stratum that are almost double those in the upper stratum. This suggests that diversification into non-farm activities is not the only livelihood diversification strategy among lower stratum house-

---

[2] Collection of data on landholdings followed the method used by Matlon (1977), which involved detailed discussions with each landholding household member (including women) concerning the proportionate relationship of each holding to the member's largest farm, followed by the actual measurement of the largest farm of each household member. This method was found by Matlon to be a reasonably accurate indication of actual holding size. In cases in which women's land was not in the village, proxies were calculated on the basis of estimates of farm sizes relative to the size of the household courtyard, which was then measured.

holds. Recourse to independent sources of agricultural income also appears to play a role in compensating for inadequate provision on the part of household heads.

Table 4.2
Average land holdings of households and household members (hectares)

Stratum	Number of households	Number of economically active members	Average household land holdings (ha.)	Average heads' land holdings (ha.)	Aver. male dependents' land holdings (ha.)*	Average women's land holdings (ha.)*
Upper	21	81	3.79	3.32	0.55 (15)	0.04 (45)
Lower	19	50	3.08	2.54	1.02 (8)	0.09 (23)
Total sample	40	131	3.45	2.95	0.72 (23)	0.05 (68)

* Figures in brackets represent numbers of male dependents and women respectively.
Source: Fieldwork 1996-97

Given repeated assertions that women in this area do not participate in farming, the fact that a share of household land holdings belongs to women may at first seem surprising. Contrary to the general perception concerning African women's access to land, Muslim Hausa women can and do own land, despite the fact that the majority of them do not farm. Under Islam, women have the right to inherit land, though they are entitled to only one half the share enjoyed by their male relatives. However, gender differences in land holdings in Nasarawan Doya were found to be extremely wide. Men controlled 97% of the land in the sample, while women had only 3%. Less than 20% of the women in the sample owned land, and the bulk of it inherited (Table 4.3).[3] The holdings of women who did own land were tiny, averaging just 0.28 ha. In most cases, women's land was left in the care of male relatives, who farmed it and sometimes gave a share of the produce to

---

[3]   It should be noted that, in view of the very early age of marriage in Hausa Muslim society, a significant percentage of the women were not yet eligible to inherit land because their parents were still alive.

the owner. This was not entirely an expression of male domination. In fact, previous studies, as well as interviews with informants in Nasarawan Doya, indicate that, since the value of land began to increase in the 1970s, women in this area now go to greater lengths to obtain their share of inherited land, even to the point of going to court (Meagher 1991; Ross 1987). However, having obtained recognition of their share, most women leave the land with their male relatives, in order to maintain a stronger claim on the resources of their male kin in times of trouble.

Table 4.3
Women's land holdings and forms of tenure

Stratum	Average land holding (ha.)	% who own land	% of land inherited	% of land purchased	% of land other
Upper	0.04	20	87	0	13
Lower	0.09	19	33	50	17
Sample average	0.05	19	72	15	13

Source: Fieldwork 1996-97

Only two of the 68 women in the sample actually farmed, and both of them belonged to the lower stratum of households, which accounts for the larger average land holdings among lower-stratum women. One of the two farming women belonged to the Christian household in the sample, and was not subject to Islamic constraints on agricultural participation. In fact, among the Christian and pagan Hausa, agriculture is one of the main economic activities of women, who have central responsibilities in household staple food provisioning. This woman owned 0.55 ha. of land, all of which she had purchased. The second woman who farmed was a particularly enterprising Muslim woman who hired labour to farm for her. She had acquired land on loan from her father, and later bought it from him, though the land amounted to only 0.07 ha.

As suggested by these last statements, the comparative equality in land holdings at the household level is not the result of an absence of land markets. In addition to traditional forms of access to land, which include inheritance (*gado*), gift (*kyauta*), borrowing (*aro*) and mortgaging (*jingina*), full blown land markets have existed since the colonial period, and have become particularly active since the 1970s. Markets exist for both purchase and rental of land. Table 4.4 shows the relative importance of these various forms of tenure in total household land holdings. While inheritance remains the dominant form of land acquisition, purchased land accounts for over one-third of the land holdings of upper stratum households, and almost 20% of the holdings of lower stratum households. Rental and borrowing of land are also widely practised, particularly among lower stratum households who are less able to afford to purchase land.

Table 4.4
Importance of various forms of land tenure

Stratum	% of land inherited	% of land purchased	% of land borrowed/rented	% of land other
Upper	43	37	12	8
Lower	53	19	21	7
Sample average	48	16	16	8

Source: Fieldwork 1996-97

The development of fairly active land markets in the area has taken place in the context of a narrowing overall access to land. Over the past two decades, Nasarawan Doya has experienced the closing of the land frontier, accompanied by significant increases in land prices. In the context of population growth, expanding opportunities in grain agriculture and significant alienation of land since the 1970s for commercial and institutional uses, the village's land surplus has been exhausted. There is no unowned land under the jurisdiction of the Village Head, and acquisition of land through communal allocation is no longer an option. The only land that remains unowned is that belonging to the forest reserve that occupies part of the traditional land area of the village. However, land from the forest reserve can only be allocated by the State government, and therefore requires significant political connections. Thus, for the vast majority of villagers, purchase remains the only means of permanently acquiring additional land At the time of study, one hectare of farm land in Nasarawan Doya cost about N10,000 (US$ 112.00), which dramatically exceeds the disposable income of most households. While this has not yet become a significant constraint on agricultural production, it is likely to become a significant issue in succeeding generations.

Land rental is more affordable than purchase, and is widely practised, particularly among lower stratum households. Renting a hectare of land cost approximately N200 ($ 2.35) per season in 1997, though the owner also demanded a token portion of the produce as a gesture of recognition that the land has only been rented, not sold. However, as land becomes more scarce and costly to buy, land owners have become more reluctant to rent out land, except to relatives, for fear that the tenant may try to lay permanent claim to the land. Since 1995, there has been an increase in the availability of land for rent owing to the high cost and scarcity of fertilizer. But the availability of this uncultivated land for rent remains constrained by the concern of owners to avoid the risk of subsequent ownership claims on the part of tenants. The result has been to moderate any increases in the cost of renting land, while continuing to limit access.

In the face of growing land pressure and the widespread use of chemical fertilizers, the practice of fallowing land has declined significantly (Matlon 1979; Mustapha 1990). This has important implications for soil fertility, which has been showing signs of stress throughout the grain surplus region for some years (Mustapha & Meagher 1992). It is currently estimated that no more than 10% of village land is left uncultivated, and the major reason is lack of fertilizer rather than a deliberate decision to fallow. In the house-hold sub-sample, only 5% of total land was left uncultivated in the 1996/7 agricultural year, and more than half of those with uncultivated land cited the lack of fertilizer as the reason for the failure to cultivate. Thus, in addition to growing concerns about the quantity of land that will be available to households in future, there are also growing concerns about the quality of land.

To recap the land argument, inequality in land holdings is not, as yet, a significant factor in agricultural inequality. Nor is land shortage important as a pressure for diversification into non-farm activities, at least not at the household level. But current trends in access to land and in quality of land (soil fertility) suggest that land shortage is likely to become a problem in the village over the next generation. While this analysis would suggest that poorer households, who are less able to buy additional land, are more likely to be forced to turn to non-farm activities for additional income, disaggregated data on the land holdings of household members suggests a different reading of the situation. In lower stratum households, dependent males and women make greater efforts to acquire land than dependants in upper stratum households. Keeping a foothold in agriculture clearly remains more central to the livelihood strategies of dependents in lower stratum households than those in upper stratum households.

Inputs, crop prices and cropping choices

While land has not, as yet, become a major constraint on agricultural production, access to sufficient capital and inputs to cultivate available land has become increasingly problematic. The predominance of a capital rather than a land constraint has long been recognized as a feature of Hausa agriculture (Hill 1972). However, the intensity of the capital constraint has become particularly pronounced in the context of Nigeria's Structural Adjustment Programme in 1986. Currency devaluation and the liberalization of crop prices, in conjunction with the imposition of bans on the importation of rice and maize in 1985, wheat in 1986, and barley in 1988, have brought about spectacular increases in the prices of local crops. In the decade between 1985 and 1995, the prices of maize and sorghum (important industrial as well as consumer substitutes for wheat and barley, as well as being the two most important cash crops in Nasarawan Doya over the period), increased by over 1,500% and 1,200%, respectively. Unfortunately, since the end of the 1980s, the progressive removal of subsidies on agricultural inputs, in conjunction with currency devaluation, has led to even more rapid increases in the prices of fertilizer and pesticides, the two main agricultural inputs in savanna agriculture (Meagher 1994).

From 1995, increases in fertilizer prices further intensified as a result of a ban imposed in 1995 on the importation of fertilizer (with a view to stimulating local fertilizer production). Access to fertilizer was worsened in 1996 by the strict enforcement of a long-standing, but widely ignored, ban on the distribution of fertilizer through the open market. This led to a crisis in access to fertilizer during the critical phase of the 1996/7 cropping season. In the face of these measures, fertilizer prices more than doubled between 1995 and 1996. At the same time, increases in grain prices have been dampened by the removal of bans and reduction of tariffs on imported wheat (1992) and rice (1995 and 1997), and the progressive relaxing of the ban on maize imports. The result was increased exposure of grain producers to competition from cheaper foreign substitutes from 1993 on, both in food consumption and in local agro-industry. The devaluation of the CFA Franc in 1994 compounded the pressure on local grain prices by undermining the previously lucrative cross-border grain trade to Niger and Chad (Meagher et al. 1996). The result has been the progressive erosion of the profitability of several of the main cash crops of the Nigerian savanna, compounded by a dizzying instability in crop price movements.

Table 4.5 compares indices of local grain prices with the price of fertilizer (the main input in savanna grain production), and the rural cost of living in Nigeria. Fertilizer price indices refer to the open market price, which is the distribution channel through which the vast majority of northern Nigerian farmers procure their fertilizer. The grain price indices for maize and sorghum refer to wholesale prices in Makarfi market, the rural bulking market in which most farmers in Nasarawan Doya market their crops. Clearly, since 1992 (the year of the unbanning of wheat imports) grain price increases have been significantly outstripped by increases in both fertilizer prices and the rural cost of living, leading to a significant decline in real agricultural incomes. Price relationships between cowpeas/groundnuts and pesticides have suffered from the same problem (Meagher 1995; KTARDA 1989; 1993)

Among poor farming households, the dramatic increase in grain prices poses serious difficulties independent of movements in input costs. Even in the savanna grain belt, a significant proportion of farming households are unable to meet their annual subsistence food needs. In Nasarawan Doya, 18% of household heads had to buy staple food for their household in 1996/7. For these households, and for others who hover on the edge of food self-sufficiency in a climate of uncertain rainfall, high grain prices constitute a serious threat to livelihoods.

Table 4.5
Price indices for fertilizer, grains and the rural cost of living, 1991-95 (1985 = 100)

Year	Fertilizer (market price)	Maize	Sorghum	Rural CPI
1991	389	348	337	328
1992	767	563	524	471
1993	1389	654	517	737
1994	1333	578	512	1154
1995	4444	1621	1340	2022

Sources: APMEU unpublished grain price data; Central Bank of Nigeria, *Annual Report and Statement of Accounts* 1988-92; Egg & Igue 1993; KTARDA Quarterly and Annual Reports 1990-92; Meagher 1991.

This range of economic pressures on agriculture have significantly affected both the types of crops grown and the absolute level of crop production. As recently as the early 1990s, hybrid maize was one of the most important cash crops in the region around Nasarawan Doya, particularly among the top stratum of farmers, significantly outstripping marketed production of sorghum. However, maize is particularly dependent on chemical fertilizer. The rising cost and declining access to fertilizer has forced farmer in all socio-economic categories to cut back on maize production. In fact, during the fertilizer crisis of 1996, some farmers in Nasarawan Doya who had planted in anticipation of fertilizer, uprooted the germinating maize from their fields and replaced it with other crops. The same practice was observed in a number of other farming communities in the maize producing region.

While the shift away from maize production has been particularly marked since the surge in fertilizer prices in 1995, a trend away from maize production, particularly among small-scale farmers, has been observed since the early 1990s (Meagher & Ogunwale 1994; KTARDA 1993). This has prompted not so much a shift out of agriculture, as a shift in favour of alternative cash crops which are less input dependent. Principal among these in Nasarawan Doya are sorghum, which is also the region's major staple, sugar cane, peppers and rice (Table 4.6). Even among these crops, fertilizer is important for good yields, but, unlike maize, some gain over the initial investment can be obtained even with little or no fertilizer.

Table 4.6
Percent share of major cash crops in total crop income (1996/7 cropping season)

Stratum	Sorghum	Sugar cane	Maize	Peppers	Rice	Ground-nut	Cowpea	Other
Upper	26	20	14	14	14	4	3	5
Lower	23	22	13	12	15	6	4	5
Sample average	25	20	14	14	14	5	3	5

Source: Fieldwork 1996-97

In 1996/7, the two most important cash crops in Nasarawan Doya were sorghum and sugar cane, which accounted for 26% and 20%, respectively of total income from marketed crops. While sorghum has been a central food and cash crop for years, the prominence of sugar cane as a cash crop represents, at least in part, a response to commercial opportunities created by structural adjustment. While sugar cane has always been a significant cash crop in the area, particularly among wealthy farmers, it has benefited from rising prices under structural adjustment owing to increased demand for locally produced sugar as a substitute for imported granulated sugar. The resulting shift toward sugar cane production has also involved a shift in the variety of sugar cane produced. Over the past decade, the variety introduced (often under duress) during the colonial period for industrial sugar production has been abandoned in favour of a more traditional local variety suited for artisanal sugar production.

In the context of wide access to river bottom land (*fadama*) required for sugar cane production, both upper and lower-stratum households in Nasarawan Doya have gone into sugar cane production. Average *fadama* holdings represent 0.72 ha. in upper-stratum households, and 0.50 ha. in lower-stratum households, which in both cases comprises 17% of total land holdings. It was found that 68% of the households grew sugar cane in the 1996 cropping year, with a slight bias toward upper stratum households. This reflects the greater ability of upper stratum households to exploit new opportunities in sugar cane production, owing to greater access to *fadama* land, and a greater ability to afford at least some fertilizer. However, a much stronger bias in favour of upper-stratum households is reflected in the levels of commercialization of sugar cane. While lower-stratum households marketed 93% of their sugar cane, upper-stratum households marketed only 66%, and processed most of the remainder in household-based sugar production enterprises. The ability to engage in local sugar production, which has a comparatively high capital threshold, considerably improves the profitability of sugar cane production.

The profitability of pepper production has also enjoyed sporadic improvements under structural adjustment. A surge in pepper prices during the early 1990s brought windfall profits to many local farmers. In the case of one farmer interviewed, profits from pepper production were invested in the purchase of a horse and sugar cane crushing machine for the production of local sugar.

Despite the creation of a few cash cropping opportunities, the realignment of input and crop prices under structural adjustment has led to an overall decline in agricultural production. While the early years of structural adjustment were reckoned by many farmers to have increased the profitability of farming, most of the farmers interviewed indicated that they had been forced to cut back on their level of agricultural production over the past two years owing to the high cost and unavailability of fertilizer. Studies conducted in other villages in the area suggest that, particularly among small-scale farmers, levels of agricultural production have been under pressure since the early 1990s, particularly among the lower stratum of farmers (Meagher & Ogunwale 1994).

High fertilizer prices also appeared to have depressed the levels of crop marketing. In both the 1995 and the 1996 agricultural years, sample households marketed an average of only 50% of total crop production, in both upper and lower-stratum households. Studies of another village in the area in the early 1990s indicate levels of commercialization of the order of 60% (Meagher 1991). In upper-stratum households, the lower levels of commercialization reflect in part the shift to the production of sugar cane for processing into local sugar rather than for direct marketing. However, high fertilizer costs also appear to have encouraged some farming households to hold back some of their surplus grain production in the hope of more remunerative grain prices.

Perceptions of agricultural constraints and prospects

Interviews with older members of the community suggested that local assessments of the overall performance and prospects of farming since Independence were mixed. On the one hand, the introduction during the 1970s of improved inputs and new crops, principally maize and cowpeas, and the extensive development of local as well as regional agricultural markets, appears to have made agriculture more profitable. On the other hand, a number of older men argued that agriculture, though more profitable, was less productive than before the introduction of fertilizers. It was felt that the soil yielded more in the late colonial period, and that, even with the help of chemical fertilizer, the land had become less productive than it used to be. The declining productivity of the land was attributed to various causes, including less reliable rainfall, the decline in fallowing, and the introduction of chemical fertilizers, which were felt by some to have 'weakened' the soil.

Older members of the community also felt that agriculture had suffered from a breakdown in the traditional household organization of labour. Since the early 1970s, sons have left the household production unit (*gandu*) earlier, weakening household control over agricultural labour, particularly among low-income households who are less able to hire labour from outside the household. This trend is corroborated by evidence from earlier studies of the breakdown of *gandu* labour units in rural Hausaland (Wallace 1978). The tendency of young men to withdraw earlier from *gandu* was attributed by older men to the disrespectful nature and laziness of modern youth, who were unwilling to engage in hard work. It was felt that young men now left the household farm to engage in non-farm activities, not because of a lack of land or capital, but because non-farm activities were less arduous than farming.

Interviews with household heads as well as dependents concerning more recent trends in agricultural prospects revealed concerns that centred around lack of access to fertilizer and the closing of the land frontier. However, perceptions of agricultural constraints varied importantly according to gender, generation and socio-economic status.

In the sub-sample, household members were asked to indicate whether access to land, labour or capital constituted important constraints on the expansion of their farming activities. Over 80% of household heads ranked access to capital as the most important constraint on agricultural production, owing to a combination of rising production and household maintenance costs. 70% of women, including the two who farmed, also identified access to capital as their most serious constraint, although the vast majority indicated that even with greater access to capital, they would not engage in farming because it was 'not their tradition'. By contrast, 52% of male dependents claimed that land, rather than capital, was their most serious agricultural constraint, while 48% stated that their most serious agricultural constraint was capital. It is worth noting that three-quarters of the male dependents who identified land as the most critical constraint belonged to the lower stratum of households, while the primary concern with capital was biased toward upper-stratum youths.

The two major solutions for coping with the capital constraint were to cut back on household expenditure and to cut back on agricultural production. In the case of the land constraint, the solutions proffered involved, for household heads, managing the little land one had or renting land, while for male dependents the overwhelming solution involved finding ways to earn money to buy land. Interestingly, non-farm activities, especially agricultural wage labour, were listed by young men as one of the major sources of income for buying land. This suggests an alternative to the 'laziness' interpretation offered by older males regarding the tendency of young men to leave the household production units in pursuit of a range of non-farm activities.

The perceptions of household members concerning the major constraints faced in agriculture are surprising in three respects. First of all, out of the 133 household members interviewed, only one respondent, a household head, identified access to labour as a constraint on agriculture, which challenges the conventional notion of African agriculture as primarily labour constrained. In Nasarawan Doya, the supply of agricultural labour has been swelled over the past decade by increasingly harsh economic and environmental conditions in the drier agricultural areas to the north, as well as by the increasingly active participation of local youth and low-income household heads in agricultural wage labour in order to meet up with the rising cost of inputs, food and land. This appears to have dampened real increases in the cost of labour relative to increases in land and input costs.

A second surprise is that land was perceived to be such a serious constraint among the youth. Over half of the male dependents, but only 7% of household heads, identified access to land as their most serious problem. This supports earlier evidence of the recent emergence of a land constraint in Nasarawan Doya, once again contradicting the conventional land surplus image of African, as well as northern Nigerian, agriculture.

A third surprise is that none of the women, not even those who farmed, identified access to land as an important constraint on their agricultural activities. Although women's access to land is quite limited, it was not perceived by women themselves to be a significant constraint on their more active participation in agriculture. Traditional norms, and lack of capital, were identified as the major limiting factors, and there was little indication of a desire to alter these norms or to deploy any increase in access to capital in agricultural activities.

Despite the perception of serious constraints on agricultural production, and solutions that depended heavily on reducing expenditure or reducing levels of agricultural production, perceptions of the future prospects of agriculture in the area were remarkably sanguine. 89% of household heads felt that agriculture remained promising, though 66% indicated that the promise of agriculture was conditional on access to fertilizer. 11% felt that farming had actually become more productive or profitable. Only 9% of household heads felt that agriculture was not promising. It is worth noting that the average age of the agricultural pessimists was 38 years, and two thirds of them were under 40. This suggests that, among men, access to land plays a key role in perceptions about the future of agriculture as a source of livelihood.

Pull factors: Household characteristics, non-farm participation and rural inequality

The complex of socio-economic, gender and generational factors that structure the impact of push factors out of agriculture also play a key role in structuring access to non-farm incomes. In Nasarawan Doya, however, it is those groups who are most disadvantaged by their position in the agricultural economy who are least able to gain advantageous access to the non-farm sector. This means that patterns of non-farm participation have tended to increase rather than moderate economic inequalities arising from agriculture. Recent non-farm literature identifies gender, access to capital, household composition, education and skills as important characteristics in determining access to non-farm incomes (Gordon 1999; Reardon et al. 1998). Evidence to assess the impact of these factors on non-farm participation will be drawn from the main sample of household heads, which permits an analysis of three strata rather than the two strata available in the sub-sample.

As mentioned above, gender is not a significant factor at the household level (gender of head), though it plays a significant role in limiting access to adequate non-farm incomes at the individual level through the influence of wife-seclusion and the gender division of labour operating within the non-farm sector. Regarding access to capital, both Gordon and Reardon et al. recognize that agricultural assets play a central role in the financing of non-farm start-ups, but they consider land to be the key factor. In Nasarawan Doya, however, land is not a significant source of non-farm capital as will be discussed in more detail below. The key factor in access to non-farm capital is crop-sales, which, as shown in Table 4.1 above, are highly biased in favour of the upper stratum of households.

As regards household composition, household size, number of wives and number of migrants per household are important indicators of the labour available for participation in non-farm activities. Table 4.7 shows that upper stratum households, who hire in more than 90% of the labour they use on the household farm, also have the largest average household size, at 13.5 members. This suggests a high level of labour available for participation in the non-farm sector. Conversely, lower stratum households, who perform most of their own agricultural labour and also hire out labour to other house-holds, have sizes averaging less than half the size of those in the upper stratum, leaving them with significantly less surplus labour available for non-farm participation.

Table 4.7
Aspects of household composition that influence access to non-farm incomes

Stratum	Age of head	Household size	No. of wives	No. of migrants
Upper	48.1	13.5	1.9	0.41
Middle	43.7	10.4	2.0	0.07
Lower	37.1	6.4	1.4	0.02
Sample average	40.7	8.6	1.7	0.07

Source: Fieldwork 1996-97

The number of wives per household head has a more direct influence on household levels of non-farm participation. While Islam allows a man to marry up to four wives, the ability to acquire additional wives is based on wealth, and few rural dwellers in northern Nigeria are able to marry more than two. While upper stratum households in the sample have an average of 1.9 wives, lower stratum households have only 1.4. Most wives in rural northern Nigeria earn incomes, but the practice of wife seclusion restricts them almost exclusively to non-farm activities. Thus, better-off households tend to have more wives, which translates on average into more non-farm incomes.

The average number of migrants per household is a further indicator of access to non-farm incomes via remittances. The table shows a sharp differentiation in access to such remittance incomes. While upper stratum households have a migrant member for every two and a half households, this drops sharply in the case of middle stratum households, who have only seven migrants per 100 households, and falls to only two migrants per 100 households in the case of lower stratum households.

An age variable has been included to consider the possible influence of life-cycle factors on variations in household composition and non-farm participation. The fact that upper stratum households are not only larger, but have heads who are on average older suggests that life-cycle factors do play a role. However, the variation in average age of household heads is only 11 years, while the heads interviewed ranged from young men in their early twenties to old men in their seventies. Moreover, household size was found to be more strongly correlated with labour stratum than with age, and the correlation with labour stratum was found to be significant, while that with age was not (see Appendix).

As Table 4.8 indicates, superior access to financing and labour in the upper stratum has resulted in higher levels of non-farm participation. Overall, 88% of household heads recognized themselves as practitioners of non-farm activities (although in the course of actual activity monitoring, the figure was found to be higher). Disaggregating by economic stratum, all household heads in the upper stratum had some type of non-farm activity. Household heads with no non-farm activities were heavily concentrated in the two lower socio-economic strata, three-quarters of them in the lowest stratum.

In many cases, household heads pursued more than one non-farm activity, and additional non-farm activities were pursued by other family members, especially wives. The number of activities per household head, and per household, were positively correlated with socio-economic status. Households in the upper stratum had an average of 5.0 non-farm activities,

Table 4.8
Participation in non-farm activities

Stratum	% of heads participating in non-farm activities	Mean no. of non-farm activities per head	Mean no. of non-farm activities per household
Upper	100.0	1.8	5.0
Middle	92.8	1.2	4.0
Lower	82.3	1.3	2.9
Sample average	88.0	1.3	3.5

Source: Fieldwork 1996-97

while those in the middle and lower stratum averaged 4.0 and 2.9 activities, respectively. Clearly the greater number of wives and larger households in middle and upper-stratum households contributes to the greater number of non-farm activities, but the underlying capacity to acquire more wives, and to start-up more non-farm activities suggests the importance of economic factors.

Control of agricultural and non-agricultural assets tends to support this assessment. Although the upper stratum accounted for only 7% of the sample, its members owned 27% of the livestock, 40% of the ploughs and threshing machines, 44% of the residential plots, 26% of the motorized transport (though only 10% of the bicycles). The bias in equipment for lucrative non-farm activities was equally great. The upper stratum owned 50% of the grinding machines, 19% of the sugar cane crushing machines, 38% of the sewing machines, and 25% of the macaroni machines. By contrast, the lower stratum, which comprised 51% of the sample, owned 27% of the livestock, 10% of the ploughs and threshing machines, 12% of the residential plots, 30% of the motorized transport, and 34% of the bicycles. The lower stratum performed even worse in terms of access to equipment for lucrative non-farm activities. They owned none of the grinding machines, 21% of the sugar cane crushing machines, 12% of the sewing machines, and 25% of the macaroni machines.

While this static picture of the distribution of assets suggests a significant degree of inequality, it does not indicate whether this represents a process of differentiation or a more cyclical pattern of inter-household inequalities. In order to gain a more longitudinal picture of patterns of asset distribution, household heads were asked to indicate whether they had more or fewer of certain key assets than their fathers had at the same stage in life.

The question of heads' asset ownership relative to that of their fathers was posed with regard to land, livestock and 'other' assets, which refers to the range of real estate, vehicles and equipment discussed above. In order to minimize the extent to which the answer to one question would bias the answer to the other, the questions were posed at widely different points in the interview, in each case, following an extensive discussion concerning the respondent's own control of the asset in question.

Table 4.9
Household heads' perceptions of inter-generational accumulation of key economic assets (% of household heads)

Stratum	Land holdings relative to father		Livestock holdings relative to father		Other asset holdings relative to father	
	More	Less	More	Less	More	Less
Age Middle	57.1	10.0	52.4	19.0	54.8	9.5
Lower	33.3	39.2	33.3	27.5	47.1	11.8
Sample average	46.0	30.0	43.0	24.0	53.0	10.0

Source: Fieldwork 1996-97

The responses, represented in Table 4.9, show a strong tendency toward inter-generational accumulation in the upper stratum, and a more moderate trend toward accumulation in the middle stratum. By contrast, the lower stratum shows a stronger tendency toward stagnation and declining control of resources, especially in the case of land. While nearly three-quarters of the upper stratum claimed to own more land than their fathers at the same stage in life, barely one-third of the lower stratum claimed to own more land than their fathers, and 39% claimed to own less.

The trend toward differentiation in livestock ownership appears somewhat more moderate. Only 57% of the upper stratum claimed to own more livestock than their fathers, against 33% in the lower stratum, and the percentages who claimed to own less livestock are on average lower than in the case of land. In the case of other assets, there is a pronounced trend toward accumulation in all strata, with nearly 50% or more of each stratum owning more than their fathers, and barely 10% or less in any given stratum owning less. However, this is less an indicator of improvements in socio-economic position than of the rapid technological, social and economic change experienced over the past generation. The commercialization of crop production, and penetration of consumer durables into rural northern Nigeria have both expanded dramatically since the 1960s, making assets such as bicycles and radios, which were extremely uncommon among the previous generation of household heads, commonplace in the current generation.

The information presented above tends to corroborate evidence of a positive association between agricultural inequality and inequalities in access to non-farm incomes in the African context. Inequalities in access to agricultural resources translate directly into inequalities in access to capital, labour and assets necessary for advantageous entry into the non-farm sector. However, there were two key household assets that were not found to be strongly associated with agricultural inequalities, nor with significant inequalities in access to non-farm incomes: land and education. The issue of land has already been discussed in some detail, but the comparative unimportance of education in the region remains to be clarified.

In contrast to many parts of Africa, education currently plays a very limited role in the determination of inequalities in access to non-farm incomes within northern Nigerian rural communities. It does, however, play a critical role in structuring regional inequalities in access to skilled non-farm employment, from which the bulk of rural Muslim northerners are excluded because of their lack of educational attainment. The explanation derives from the historical friction between Islamic social and political institutions and the Western (Christian) education system, a friction reinforced by the colonial system of indirect rule. The Muslim majority of rural dwellers throughout the savanna tend to adhere to the pre-existing Koranic education system, which does little to improve access to jobs in the modern sector. Among household heads in Nasarawan Doya, 88% had Koranic education, but only 7% had any exposure to primary education, and a mere 2% had some secondary education. While primary education was positively associated with socio-economic status, the two household heads with some secondary education were both young men in the lowest socio-economic stratum. Evidence from the household sub-sample suggests that generational and gender factors are important determinants of access to Western education, which is most strongly associated with young males. All of the wives and female dependents had Koranic or no education. By contrast, 34% of the economically active male dependents (all of whom were under 25) had primary education. This suggests that education is likely to become more significant as a determinant of non-farm income inequality in the coming generation. However, the increasing monetisation of access to education under structural adjustment, and the near-collapse of local primary provision, is reinforcing a bias of educational attainment toward better-off households.

The incidence of technical skills outside of agriculture was also found to be fairly low. Among household heads in the main sample, 5% had some mechanical skills (mostly bicycle repair), 4% had some training in tailoring, and 2% had training in local building crafts. Tailoring skills were biased toward the top stratum, mechanical skills were concentrated in the middle stratum, and traditional skills were entirely in the lower stratum. Clearly literacy in the colonial tongue and access to capital are important determinants of inequalities in skill acquisition. The lack of literacy in English in particular has retarded the development of apprenticeship systems in modern skilled activities such as electronic and mechanical repairs, which have become highly developed among other Nigerian ethnic groups.

The preceding analysis suggests a growing tension, rather than a complementarity, between the push and pull factors that determine patterns of non-farm participation. Evidence of the range of serious economic pressures arising within agriculture – on access to land and inputs, on the profitability of grain production, and on household provisioning – is indicative of some of the major forces encouraging a recourse to non-farm sources of income. However, the evidence presented above has shown that it is the better-off households least affected by these 'push' factors, that tend to have the greatest propensity to diversify into non-farm activities. Conversely, the rural poor, who experience the greatest 'push' out of agriculture, lack the resources to gain adequate access to non-farm alternatives. The next section will consider how these tensions are playing themselves out within the context of the non-farm sector. How do the more intensive 'push' factors faced by the rural poor, and their comparative lack of 'pull' factors, affect their terms of entry into the non-farm sector? To what extent, and for which groups, does the non-farm sector provide resources for improved livelihoods and increases in agricultural investment? How has the process of economic restructuring affected the profitability of non-farm activities? These questions will be addressed within the context of a detailed historical and sociological analysis of the non-farm sector in the Nigerian savanna.

5

Non-farm activities and structural adjustment: An enterprise perspective

The rural non-farm sector is often portrayed as a relatively static sector, little affected by economic change, dominated by locals and serving essentially local markets. The development of the non-farm sector in Nasarawan Doya has been characterized by a comparatively high degree of mobility and adaptation to social, political and economic change. Over the long term, it is a history that reflects the decline of many traditional non-farm activities and the rise of new opportunities. Under the impact of structural adjustment, the structure of economic pressures and opportunities has changed yet again, undermining the profitability of some non-farm activities as well as creating some new non-farm opportunities. Beginning with a history of non-farm activities in Nasarawan Doya, this section will explore the effect of structural adjustment on the operation of a sample of 50 local non-farm enterprises.

The history of non-farm activities in Nasarawan Doya

By the beginning of the colonial period, a fairly wide range of non-farm activities were already practised in Nasarawan Doya. These ranged from local crafts for the production of household goods (pottery, calabash repairs and mat making) and textiles (weaving, tailoring and embroidery), to the activities of semi-occupational castes, including blacksmiths, butchers and traditional barbers. Trade was also an important activity, both regional grain trade to Zaria, and long distance trade in donkey caravans to places as far as Maiduguri and Lagos, for the purchase of kola, earrings, potash, rope and needles (see Hill 1977; Baier 1980). However, participation in long-distance trade was quite limited, with only a few traders per year travelling out from Nasarawan Doya. Right up through the early colonial period, there was little in the way of wage labour. Villagers had no money to hire labour, and traditional as well as colonial officials tended to rely more on corvee and forced labour.

Although a range of non-farm activities existed, they played a relatively limited role in the village economy during this early period. The need for money was confined largely to official obligations, such as tax payments and donations for village activities. Non-farm activities were confined essentially to the dry season. During the wet season, villagers spent much more time on the farm, often returning late in the evening, rather than in the afternoon as they do now. (One might wonder to what extent the earlier return from the farm could be attributed to the advent of bicycles and motorcycles, rather than to reduced concentration on agriculture.)

The major changes in the non-farm sector during the colonial period revolved around the destruction of local crafts, the introduction of female seclusion, and the penetration of new activities. In Nasarawan Doya, crafts such as mat making, pottery, spinning, and weaving disappeared during the colonial period owing to competition from imported substitutes, and the deliberate suppression of the indigenous textile industry.

The practice of female seclusion penetrated into Nasarawan Doya during the 1930s. Previously, Muslim Hausa women had been involved in a wide range of agricultural and non-farm activities. In the outlying hamlets, women engaged in most of the same agricultural activities as men, while in the village proper, women harvested low-lying crops such as beans and peppers, and brought in the harvest. With the advent of seclusion, women gradually withdrew from these agricultural activities. This process coincided with the disappearance of local crafts, many of which were practised by women, particularly pottery, spinning and weaving. This resulted in a significant narrowing of women's economic activities to little more than crop processing, the production of snacks and condiments, and petty trade. For some time after the introduction of seclusion, some women continued to farm through the agency of hired labour, but this became increasingly uncommon from the 1970s owing to the rising cost of land, labour and inputs.

A range of new activities began to penetrate into the village from the latter half of the colonial period. Local sugar production was regarded by older men in the village as a new activity, which came into the village during the 1930s or 1940s. From the 1950s, various modern crafts and services were introduced into the village from the surrounding towns. The first modern tailor with a sewing machine was a native of Zaria city who came to Nasarawan Doya in the 1950s. Thereafter, indigenes of the village went to Zaria to learn tailoring, and returned to practise the trade in the village. The first bicycle repairman, a native of Nasarawan Doya who trained in Zaria, began practising in the village in the 1950s or 1960s. Commercial grinding machines, owned by prosperous local farmers, began to appear during the 1970s.

Also during the late colonial period, Yoruba traders began to bring imported manufactured goods to the village market to sell on credit – goods such as cloth, pots, dishes, plastic ware, palm oil and salt. They were followed by Igbo traders who brought such goods as medicine and bicycle parts, as well as basic consumer manufactures. The first resident Igbo shopkeeper came to the village in the 1980s, and others have since followed.

Employment in the formal sector has been consistently low, owing to the lack of industry in the area and the pervasive lack of Western education among local people. During the 1970s, some village indigens found employment as teachers and low-level civil servants. Opportunities for formal sector employment narrowed during the 1980s, but have increased since the early 1990s with the creation of Makarfi Local Government and the privatization of the Makarfi tollgate. Overall, however, levels of formal sector employment remain very low.

Current patterns of non-farm activities

The non-farm activities of the late 1990s are characterized by a high level of diversity, combining surviving traditional activities with a range of modern activities. Because of the nature of non-farm enterprises in the area, which involve seasonal activities as well as many activities performed within the confines of family compounds, an exact census of non-farm enterprises in the village would have involved a research project in itself. As a proxy, a survey of visible activities was conducted within the three wards of the main village, and then supplemented by information from discussions with local informants as to the less visible activities. This was used as a basis for the selection of a stratified sample of 50 enterprises, which targeted two to three of each of the major activities represented in the survey, depending on their numerical importance. 'Major' was defined to mean either numerous or economically prominent. Where relevant, the selection targeted a large-scale and small-scale enterprise in each category.

Overall, the enterprise sample contained 15 female-headed enterprises, and 35 male-headed enterprises. The sample was stratified economically on the basis of the current capital costs of starting up such an enterprise. Those that would cost N 2,000 (US\$ 23.53) or less to start up were grouped in the lower stratum, while those that cost over N 2,000 to start up were grouped in upper stratum. Current start-up capital for lower-stratum enterprises averaged N584 (US\$ 6.87), while that of upper-stratum enterprises averaged N 31,760 (US\$ 373.65). 50% of the enterprises fell into upper stratum, and 50% into the lower. This symmetrical distribution was not by design, although the effort to include large and small-scale representatives of various types of enterprises undoubtedly contributed to this symmetry, which represents a significant over-representation of upper-stratum enterprises within the population. 80% of the female-headed enterprises were in the lower stratum, compared to only 37% of the male enterprises. Table 5.1 indicates the share of the major enterprise categories in the sample, along with their gender and socio-economic bias.

Table 5.1
The composition of the enterprise sample

Enterprise category	% in category	% from upper stratum	% female-headed
Low income traditional crafts	0	0	0
High income traditional crafts	4	2	0
Traditional religion and medicine	4	0	0
Food and beverages	16	2	14
Agricultural processing	14	10	4
Clothing, hair & related services	10	10	4
Carpentry and modern building	2	2	0
Modern crafts and services	8	2	0
Transport	8	6	0
Retail and petty trade	8	2	6
Wholesalers and shopkeepers	12	12	2
Civil service	0	0	0
Formal sector wage labour	0	0	0
Informal wage labour (non-agricultural)*	6	2	0
Agricultural wage labour	8	0	0
Sample total	100	50	30

* The main activity in this category is wage labour for local sugar production.
Source: Fieldwork 1996-97

Just over one half of the enterprises in the sample were established since the onset of adjustment in 1986, and 26% since 1992, the beginning of the downturn in terms of trade in grain production. Only 68% of the enterprises were owned by indigenes of Nasarawan Doya. Among the non-indigenous enterprise heads, over 80% were from Hausa-Fulani or culturally similar Muslim groups from other parts of northern Nigeria and Niger Republic, all of whom operated enterprises in the lower stratum. The remaining group of non-indigenes, amounting to 6% of the total sample, were all Igbos from south-eastern Nigeria, and all operated enterprises in the upper stratum. The majority of the non-indigenes came to Nasarawan Doya after the imposition of structural adjustment in 1986.

This data is reflective of the existence of a four-way division of labour in non-farm activities, among men, women, non-indigenes from other parts of the north, and non-indigenes from southern Nigeria. Local men engage in a range of traditional male crafts, modern craft and services, male agricultural processing activities, transport activities, retail and wholesale trade, and various forms of wage labour. Local women are confined largely to activities deemed compatible with their domestic and secluded role, such as snack and food production, crop processing, petty trade and tailoring of women's clothes. 'Strangers' from other parts of northern Nigeria and Niger come to the village as agricultural and casual wage labourers, tinkers, and other such itinerant activities, while strangers from southern Nigeria continue to dominate the retail trade in manufactured goods, such as provisions and medicines.

All of the enterprises in the sample were located in Nasarawan Doya, though two of them were branches of other enterprises located in nearby towns and villages. 12% of the enterprises had moved to Nasarawan Doya from a previous location, though all of them were run by non-indigenes largely from other parts of northern Nigeria, and fell overwhelmingly in the lower stratum of enterprises. This is consistent with the observation made above that strangers from other parts of the north predominate in largely itinerant, low-income activities. In most of these cases, including those opening branches of other enterprises, the direction of enterprise movement was from larger to smaller centres. This coincided with the more general perceptions of non-farm operators themselves, who were more aware of enterprises moving to the village from the towns, than moving out to the towns from the village.

Regarding the location of their commercial activities within the village, 38% operated from their homes, most of them in the lower stratum, 16% operated in shops, all in the upper stratum, 20% conducted their activity in an open space in the village, 12% on farms, and the rest in assorted locations, including the market.

The enterprise sample reflected a relatively low level of access to education and skill formation. The educational profile showed that 86% of the operators had Koranic or no education, and only 8% had some primary education or higher, including one operator with tertiary education. The remaining 4% classified themselves as 'other'. All of those with primary education or higher operated enterprises in the top stratum. This involved a majority of locals and one operator from south-eastern Nigeria. 28% of the sample had done some form of apprenticeship, 16% of them in the upper stratum of enterprises. This tends to confirm earlier evidence of the comparative lack of education in the village, as well as the positive association of education and skill levels with higher income non-farm activities.

Many of those in the lower stratum had no previous activity, while the majority of those in the upper stratum came into their activity from farming, crafts and large-scale trade. Levels of agricultural production were positively associated with the capital level of non-farm enterprises. Among operators in the upper stratum, average agricultural production levels of the main crops were nine times the production level of operators in the lower stratum.

Interestingly, only 24% of the non-farm enterprises in the sample were seasonal, while 76% of the enterprises operated all year round, rising to 80% in the upper stratum. This challenges the persistent assumption that non-farm activities are largely seasonal in nature.

Labour and employment

Under current conditions, the contribution of non-farm activities to employment generation within the village remains fairly restricted. 54% of the enterprises in the sample were owner operated, rising to 72% in the lower stratum of enterprises, and 73% among female-headed enterprises. Levels of employment generation among the remaining enterprises that employed some additional labour were very low. Within the enterprise sample as a whole, employment in non-farm activities averaged only one additional worker (Table 5.2). Disaggregated by socio-economic stratum, the level of employment was 1.8 workers in the upper stratum and 0.4 workers in the lower stratum. Most of the labour used in these enterprises consisted of apprentices and family labour. In both cases, upper-stratum enterprises and male-headed enterprises seem significantly better able to gain access to labour than female-headed or lower-stratum enterprises.

Table 5.2
Labour use in non-farm enterprises

Enterprise category	Percent owner-operated	Average no. of employees	Average no. of apprentices	Average. no of family workers	Total average no. of workers
Upper	36	0.2	0.8	0.8	1.8
Lower	72	0.0	0.1	0.4	0.5
Male-headed	46	0.1	0.4	0.7	1.2
Female-headed	73	0.0	0.0	0.4	0.4
Sample average	54	0.1	0.3	0.6	1.0

Source: Fieldwork 1996-97

A consideration of medium-term changes in labour use suggests a somewhat more encouraging picture. According to respondents' recollections of labour use in their enterprises five years before, the use of employees has risen 150% (albeit from a very low level), all in the upper stratum of enterprises. Use of apprentices has risen by 133%, and use of family workers has risen by 200%. However, disaggregation of this data shows that lower-stratum enterprises have been less successful in increasing their total levels of employment, and among female-headed enterprise, total employment levels have actually fallen slightly.

This data indicates an overall shift in employment patterns in favour of family workers, the cheapest available type of labour. Interviews suggest that, while several enterprises in the upper stratum are felt to be more profitable, they are not sufficiently profitable to sustain a proportionate expansion in the hiring of paid employees and apprentices. Rising wage costs in the face of uncertain markets have limited the use of paid employees. Under the economic conditions of adjustment, access to and control of apprentices has also become more difficult, because of the financial pressures on apprentices to start generating their own incomes, and the high start-up costs of many of the more lucrative enterprises (see Meagher & Yunusa 1996). Within this context, the ability to control family labour has become a critical aspect of the current expansion potential of non-farm enterprises. The ability to control family labour is in turn heavily dependent on the ability to meet conventional obligations for household provisioning, particularly in terms of food, clothing and ceremonial costs, especially marriage and naming ceremonies – obligations which are becoming increasingly difficult for lower stratum operators to sustain.

Sources of capital and credit

The major supply-side factors investigated were sources of capital and credit, and access to inputs and equipment. An examination of sources of start-up capital showed agriculture to be the most important single source, accounting for start-up capital in 36% of enterprises overall, representing 56% of upper-stratum enterprises, but only 16% of lower-stratum enterprises (Table 5.3). Within the category of those who obtained their start-up capital from agricultural sources, the overwhelming majority of upper-stratum enterprises obtained it from farming (crop production and sales). By contrast, all of the lower-stratum enterprises with an agricultural source of capital obtained their capital from livestock production. This is consistent with evidence that less well-off agricultural households use most of their farm produce to meet basic household needs, and have little left over for investment in non-farm activities. Inevitably, agricultural sources of start-up capital were more important for men than for women. 43% of men obtained their start-up capital from agriculture, compared to only 20% of women, most of whom depended on livestock rather than farming.

By contrast, the sale of mortgaging of land was comparatively unimportant as a source of start-up capital. Only 2% of entrepreneurs, exclusively women in the lower stratum, were willing to endanger land holdings in this way, given that farming is not perceived as an economic option. Among men, relinquishing control of land in order to fund non-farm enterprises is not perceived as a rational economic strategy. In fact, as earlier findings suggest, the overall economic strategy is quite the reverse: young men enter into non-farm activities in order to obtain money to buy more land.

Table 5.3
Sources of start-up capital for current non-farm enterprises (% of sample)

Category	Agriculture	Assistance from rural relative	Rotating credit group	Bank loan	Sale/ mortgage of land	Other
Upper	46.0	24.0	4.0	4.0	0.0	22.0
Lower	16.0	32.0	0.0	0.0	4.0	48.0*
Male-headed	42.9	20.0	2.9	2.9	0.0	31.3
Female-headed	20.0	46.7	0.0	0.0	6.7	26.6
Sample average	36.0	28.0	2.0	02.	2.0	30.0*

* Figure includes enterprises with no start-up capital needs, which comprise 12% of entire sample.
Source: Fieldwork 1996-97

Bank loans, which may also have involved using land as collateral, were also comparatively rare. This capital source also accounted for only 2% of entrepreneurs, this time from the upper stratum, where those sufficiently well-connected for a bank loan would inevitably be located. This corroborates evidence from the household sample that crop sales, rather than land, were the key means of access to finance for non-farm start-ups.

The second most important source of start-up capital was assistance from rural relatives, which accounted for 28% of the sample. This represented the most important source of capital for female-headed enterprises, with 47% of women, compared to only 20% of men depending on this source. It was also a more important source of capital for lower-stratum enterprises. 32% of lower-stratum enterprises obtained their start-up capital from this source, compared to 24% of upper-stratum enterprises. Interestingly, none of the entrepreneurs indicated assistance from urban relatives to be a source of start-up capital, although this was included among the answer options. This is undoubtedly related to the higher cost of travelling to urban areas, which lower-stratum and female entrepreneurs are largely unable to afford.

Rotating credit groups played a predictably minor role in the provision of start-up capital, and only in the context of upper-stratum male-headed enterprises. This raises questions about the conventional assumption that rotating credit groups play an important role in funding informal economic activities among African women. Owing in part to the restrictions imposed by seclusion, rotating credit groups are not common among rural Hausa women, and, under the economic pressures of adjustment, are noted more for their collapse than for their development (Imam 1993; Meagher 2000).

'Other' sources of start-up capital constitutes a relatively large category, owing to the large proportion of non-farm activities which required no start-up capital, predominantly wage labour in various categories of agricultural and non-farm enterprises. Also included in this category were those who funded their non-farm activities from previous non-farm activities, which accounted for 6% of the sample, all male-headed upper-stratum enterprises.

Sources of capital for running non-farm enterprises showed a similar pattern of division by socio-economic stratum and by gender. 56% of upper-stratum enterprises, and 51% of men obtained the capital for running their non-farm activities largely from their non-farm profits. 44% of lower-stratum enterprises, and 80% of women, obtained their running capital from assistance from relatives or spouses.

Once an enterprise had been started up, the use of credit in its operation was surprisingly limited. 76% of the sample claimed not to use credit, rising to 80% among male-headed enterprises, and 92% among upper-stratum enterprises. However, only 46% of the sample claimed they had no need for credit. The reluctance to use credit derived largely the absence of systems of commercial credit in most activities, such that requests for credit are associated with penury. This is compounded by genuine uncertainties among entrepreneurs regarding their ability to repay in the context of unstable markets and multiple economic pressures, making them prefer to avoid credit unless forced into it by necessity. Only 18% actually said that they did not use credit because they were unable to obtain it. This was biased heavily toward lower-stratum (28%) and female-headed (33%) enterprises.

The picture that emerges from this data is one in which a large proportion of male-headed and upper-stratum enterprises got their initial capital from crop-based agriculture, and thereafter many were able to set up relatively self-sustaining non-farm enterprises. In actual fact, there is a great deal of cross-funding between agriculture and non-farm enterprises among farming entrepreneurs, owing to the economic dynamic of seasonality. This process of cross-funding is key to the viability of many non-farm enterprises, and their apparent financial independence should not mask their actual dependence on regular injections of capital or inputs from agriculture.

By contrast, female-headed and lower-stratum enterprises were heavily dependent for both start-up and running capital on various forms of assistance from spouses and rural relatives. In such enterprises, capital is regularly run down by household and unavoidable ceremonial expenses, as well as by rising costs and weakening markets, making entrepreneurial survival heavily dependent on maintaining goodwill through participation in various forms of kinship and friendship networks. While the need for credit is greater among these categories of enterprises, access to credit is severely limited by weak repayment capacity and the comparative poverty of the social networks to which these categories of non-farm operators have access.

Access to inputs and equipment

The inflationary pressures of structural adjustment have had a profoundly negative effect on the access of non-farm actors to inputs and equipment. The evidence presented above indicates that the ability to overcome inflation-induced constraints through access to credit is extremely weak. Table 5.4 shows the relationship of inflation rates for equipment, inputs, and major output of non-farm enterprises over the past five years. The data indicate that, on average, output prices have risen much more slowly than input and equipment prices, particularly in the lower stratum. Overall, equipment prices have risen by an average of 114%, input prices by 228%, while output prices have risen by only 92%. Surprisingly, female-headed enterprises appear to have fared better than other enterprise categories in keeping pace with inflation. Among lower-stratum enterprises, one third felt that they had been unable to raise their prices sufficiently to compensate for rising input costs, but nearly one half of lower stratum entrepreneurs claimed they were forced to shift to a smaller scale of operation because they could not afford to buy inputs in bulk. Among upper-stratum enterprises, 54% indicated that they had resorted to buying cheaper quality inputs or adulterating their inputs with cheaper substances in order to cope with the high cost of inputs.

Table 5.4
Inflation levels of major equipment, input, and output costs between 1992 and 1997

Enterprise category	% change in equipment costs	% change in input costs	% change in output costs
Upper	102	251	101
Lower	151	126	85
Male-headed	112	239	86
Female-headed	199	174	186
Sample average	114	228	92

Source: Fieldwork 1996-97

Similar problems arose in the case of equipment. 40% of enterprises reported problems with access to equipment. Particularly in the case of upper-stratum enterprises, the equipment required has no local equivalents. Such items as sugar cane crushing machines and certain types of mechanics tools, not to mention sewing machines and cameras, cannot be manufactured locally, since they require processes and levels of precision which are not available at the village level. 60% of upper-stratum, and 40% of lower-stratum enterprises reported that, despite the pressures of cost, they continue to acquire their equipment from nearby regional towns or urban centres, rather than opting for locally made equipment. Those who indicated they had no problems with access to equipment claimed that they had either acquired all the equipment they needed before the beginning of the structural adjustment period, or that their activity did not require costly equipment.

In attempting to cope with the high cost of equipment, the two main strategies employed by lower-stratum enterprises was to resort to local, often jerryrigged, repairs, and to downgrade their equipment use to simpler technologies. The two main strategies employed by upper-stratum enterprises was to resort to local repairs, and to buy less equipment than they needed for the activity. The implications of these adjustments for the technical level of local non-farm enterprise are not encouraging. They imply a trend toward technical regression rather than development or innovation.

Demand side factors: Competition and markets

One of the major reasons behind the inability of many enterprises to defend their output prices against inflation was the pervasive situation of intensifying competition and weakening local demand. As previous studies have indicated, the major source of demand for the output of non-farm activities in the African context comes from rural households in the village and surrounding rural area, and is heavily dependent on rising agricultural incomes (Haggblade et al. 1989; Liedholm et al. 1994; Delgado et al. 1994). In Nasarawan Doya, 80% of the enterprise sample indicated that their main customers came from local farming households, where purchasing power was far from buoyant. Only 14% derived their main source of demand from traders and other businesses with access to a wider market, and these were heavily concentrated in upper-stratum enterprises. Fisher et al. (1997) site the neglect of prevailing demand conditions as one of the central reasons for policy failure with regard to the non-farm sector.

The overwhelming importance of local consumer demand for the growth of most non-farm enterprises in Nasarawan Doya poses a dual problem. First of all, in the context of worsening terms of trade in agriculture, the local consumer market is weak. Secondly, in the context of weak local demand, the proliferation of similar types of easy-entry activities only intensifies pressures on demand. Among lower-stratum enterprises with relatively low start-up costs and low skill requirements, competition from others entering the activity was felt to place downward pressure on profits. Intensifying competition was felt to be generated largely by the increasing economic pressures on local households, creating a vicious circle of weak demand, intensifying competition and declining incomes. In interviews, operators in lower-stratum activities repeatedly complained of the lack of demand. As one female snack producer put it, capital is a problem, but even if you get the capital, there is no market. Among the majority of lower-stratum operators who felt that competition was not a problem, the reasons given were that the lack of demand prevented people from entering the activity, or that the capital costs of that particular activity were too high for most current entrants to afford.

Upper-stratum enterprises faced a somewhat different demand situation. Their higher skill levels and higher capital costs provided a certain protection from increased competition. Particularly among the better established enterprises in this category, the poorer training, equipment and workmanship of new entrants tended to protect rather than erode their market. In many other cases, the activities pursued represented a response to new non-farm opportunities opened up by adjustment, and as such, demand had increased in these activities rather than declined. 44% of upper-stratum enterprises said that they faced increased competition because the activity was profitable, and 24% said they faced no increased competition because the activity was too costly for most people to start up. In most of these cases, competition was not felt to be a problem. It is worth noting, however, that 12% of upper-stratum enterprises complained that they face increased competition from *urban* informal sector goods which are penetrating rural markets in response to the saturation of urban markets.

In the face of weak effective demand, particularly among lower-stratum and female-headed enterprises, granting credit and giving discounts to customers had become an important competitive strategy. 72% of the sample claimed to grant credit and give discounts more now than they did five years ago, rising to 76% of lower-stratum, and 87% of female-headed enterprises.

Thus, the category of enterprises least able to obtain credit and protect their profits, are those most obliged to grant credit in order to sustain their market. These competitive practices have the effect of further squeezing profits, particularly among the categories of operators who can least afford it.

Incomes and income use

The upshot of the differential impact of supply and demand pressures on non-farm enterprises is a substantial variation in income levels between upper and lower-stratum enterprises, as well as between male and female-headed enterprises. Total average profits per month for all the enterprises in the sample were N3,320 (US$ 39.00). While profits from lower-stratum enterprises averaged N1,588 (US$ 18.70) per month, those from upper-stratum enterprises averaged just over N5,000 (US$ 58.80) per month. Similarly, while women earned an average of N1,017 (US$ 12.00) per month from their non-farm activities, men earned an average of N4,306 (US$ 50.70). This indicates a significant gap between the non-farm income-generating capacity facing men and entrepreneurs with substantial capital, relative to women and entrepreneurs with minimal capital. Male earnings are over four times those of women, and earnings from upper-stratum enterprises are over three times those of lower-stratum enterprises.

The data also illustrates the very low level of incomes obtainable even from lucrative activities under current economic conditions. With fertilizer prices of N1,600 per 50 kg bag during the year of the study, and agricultural labour rates of N150 per day, the amount of agricultural investment that could be generated even by the most advantaged groups is clearly very limited. This is particularly so given the heavy pressures of rising costs of basic household necessities on non-farm outlay. Moreover, in the inflationary context of adjustment, the purchasing power of non-farm earnings was continually being undermined by rising prices. 58% of the sample maintained that their non-farm earnings did not buy as much as they did five years previously, rising to 64% of lower-stratum enterprises, and 73% of female-headed enterprises.

Given the limited purchasing power of non-farm incomes, it is not surprising that 62% of the sampled enterprises used the proceeds of their non-farm activities for consumption expenditure only, with no significant variation between enterprise strata. An additional 12% combined consumption expenditure with investment in non-farm or agricultural activities. 20% re-invested their non-farm incomes in non-farm activities, and a mere 2% invested their non-farm incomes in agriculture. All expenditure patterns which indicated any component for reinvestment in non-farm or agricultural activities were heavily biased toward the upper stratum of enterprises. This suggests that the incomes of lower-stratum enterprises are too low, and too closely associated with household survival, to allow for significant investment in productive activities.

New pressures and new opportunities in the non-farm sector

From the information presented above, it is clear that the combination of economic forces unleashed by structural adjustment has generated both winners and losers within the non-farm sector. The losers are those in activities with low barriers to entry who face intensifying competition in a context of weak or declining markets, as well as those in activities with slightly higher barriers to entry whose rising input costs have not been compensated for by commensurate increases in demand. Many categories of food and snack production, wage labour, petty trade and traditional crafts fall into this category. Unfortunately, these are also the activities that absorb the most labour within the village, particularly from the ranks of low-income households. This has clearly negative implications for the promotion of non-farm activities in the service of poverty alleviation.

The case of the village blacksmiths illustrates some of the complexities of the situation of losers in the adjustment game. From the perspective of skills, capital costs, and social barriers to entry, smithing is a highly protected activity, and it is certainly an activity in which local demand has been boosted by adjustment, owing to the increased tendency of people to resort to local repairs of tools, rather than to buy new items or take the repairs to welders or other specialists in town. But the head of the local smithing family claimed that the profitability of his smithing enterprise had declined under adjustment because of the rising cost and increasing scarcity of his major raw material, scrap metal. Over the past decade, the devaluation of the naira has intensified the recycling activities of urban industry, creating dramatic upward pressure on the cost of and urban demand for scrap metal. Largely as a result of these pressures, the blacksmith claimed that he could no longer get the metal he needed by going to Zaria. He often had to go farther afield, to Funtua, Kaduna or even Kano. The higher cost of metal, and the increased cost of finding it, had forced him to resort to buying in smaller quantities. This reduced the amount of goods he was able to produce for sale in Makarfi, the major market in the area.

Unfortunately, the pressures of rising input costs have stifled some of the blacksmith's innovative ideas. He tried his hand at producing bicycle and motorcycle carriers, but had to abandon it because the market was too weak at the village level. He was confident that these items would find a sufficient market in the town, since they are cheaper than the industrially made version, but he did not have enough capital to produce in sufficient quantity to sell in the town. He was also hampered in another area where demand for his services has been expanding: the repair of local machinery. While he can improvise some basic repairs for bicycles and motorcycles, he said he lacked the skills to repair grinding machines or any other precision machine, but declared a willingness to learn, if training was available.

This case represents the most advantaged version of the loser's scenario. It describes a fairly lucrative enterprise, protected by high skill and capital barriers to entry, and even by caste barriers. It is also an activity that has faced rising demand under structural adjustment, owing to increasing recourse of local people to repairs and local substitutes. Despite this catalogue of advantages, rising input cost were forcing a contraction in the scale of activities, and stifling innovation. Clearly, overcoming barriers to entry and increasing demand are not necessarily sufficient to stimulate enterprise growth. The effect of economic restructuring on a range of supply and demand conditions needs to be taken into consideration, not only in this case, but even more urgently in the much wider range of cases that lack the significant initial advantages outlined in this scenario.

The other side of the non-farm story is, of course, the range of new economic opportunities opened up by the realignment of economic forces under adjustment. Principal among these are local sugar production and local retailing of manufactured consumer goods. The case of local sugar production represents a situation of increased regional, rather than local, demand for an inferior good in the face of inflation and falling real incomes. Increased demand for local sugar dates from the late 1980s, a claim corroborated by the fact that 67% of those engaged in local sugar production in Nasarawan Doya entered the activity since the beginning of the adjustment period. Initially, local producers took their sugar to Makarfi market, but since the early 1990s, the demand for local sugar has increased to a point that traders from urban centres as far as Kano, Sokoto and even Minna now come into the village to purchase sugar from those who produce in sufficiently large quantity.

While local sugar production is profitable, it is also an activity with significant barriers to entry. Engagement in sugar production requires a sugar cane crushing machine and a horse, which together cost over N30,000, more than the total annual household income of some of the poorer farmers. Of even greater concern is the questionable long-term sustainability of the activity. For one thing, the sugar cane crushing machine is both imported and obsolete. The sugar machines seen in Nasarawan Doya were made in India in the 1930s. India no longer produces these machines, and no other sources of import are available – in fact, Nigeria stopped importing them in the colonial period. The machines can only be procured second-hand from farms and missions that used them during the colonial period and have since abandoned sugar production. Farmers go as far as Sokoto, Bauchi, and even Ibadan to scout for these machines, but they are becoming increasingly scarce as more and more farmers in the area turn to local sugar production. No local production of sugar cane crushing machines has as yet been undertaken, though it has been looked into. The Agricultural Mechanization Programme of the national Institute for Agricultural Research in Zaria investigated the possibility of local production of sugar machines some years ago. They found that certain parts would require casting, which they are unable to do on site, and that the cost of local production of sugar machines is unlikely to be attractive to local sugar producers. Attempts to interest the private sector have run up against the problem of uncertain markets and unprofitable relationships between production costs and effective demand.

A further problem lies in the fact that local sugar remains an inferior good. Expanding demand is based on the prevailing situation of economic hardship in the country. Should the economy improve, and real incomes begin to rise, the market for local sugar will collapse. Thus, improvements in the capacity of farmers to afford locally produced machinery will be accompanied by a decline in demand for the product of that machinery. As such, local sugar production cannot form a basis for sustainable improvements in non-farm incomes, even among wealthier households. It is only a conjunctural economic opportunity, premised on general conditions of economic hardship.

Local retail shops for consumer-manufactured goods, such as detergent, plastic ware, toiletries, and *gari* (processed cassava meal), represent another lucrative new opportunity, with similarly mixed long-term prospects. The creation of a market for local retailing of these commodities, known as 'provisions', rests, not on expanding local incomes, but on the declining consumer purchasing power. Villagers are increasingly unable to buy in sufficient quantity to justify the cost of travelling to nearby towns and urban centres to purchase basic household consumer goods, owing to rising commodity prices and transport costs. Prior to the 1990s, the few local provisions shops were the preserve of local Hausa men, who purchased goods in Makarfi and Zaria for sale in the village. Local women also engaged in some retailing and micro-retailing of provisions from within their compounds. Between the mid-1980s and the early 1990s, the one Igbo family resident in the village operated the only provisions shop owned by a non-indigen.

Since the early 1990s, however, several young Igbo men and one Yoruba have come to Nasarawan Doya to open provisions shops, a chemist, and to revive the local bakery. The impetus behind this trend is, in part, a response to the increased demand for specifically local provision of these goods, and in part a response to the lack of economic opportunities elsewhere for entrepreneurs just getting started. In interviews, the young Igbo entrepreneurs explained that many of them have been opening businesses in northern Nigerian villages because they lack the capital to open in towns. The capital threshold of opening a similar business in the urban informal sector in northern Nigerian towns and cities has risen beyond their means, and markets in southern Nigeria, both rural and urban, are saturated. Young Igbo, as well as some Yoruba, entrepreneurs are turning to medium-sized northern villages as a final commercial frontier. At this stage, the trend appears to be largely experimental – they are trying these villages out to see if there is a large enough market, but some are already complaining that demand is weak.

The impact on Hausa provisions retailers, both male and female is not yet clear. The Igbo dealers have a competitive advantage over the locals, owing the prevalence in Igbo society of strong informal commercial institutions that have laid a framework for the expansion of Igbo business networks across Nigeria, and over much of West Africa (Forrest 1994; Brautigam 1997). Central economic institutions of Igbo society include apprenticeship training in technical and commercial skills, often involving assistance with start-up capital, and home-town as well as occupational associations that provide access to discounts, suppliers' credit, and various types of loans. Such institutions are comparatively rare in Hausa society, particularly among small-scale operators in their home territory, though there are highly developed commercial networks in certain lines of business, particularly grain, livestock, kola and textiles (Baier 1980; Gregoire 1991; Hashim & Meagher 1999). Igbo networks tend to specialize in more modern activities, such as trade in manufactured and second hand goods. The result is that, in the provisions trade, young Igbo entrepreneurs have access to commercial advantages through home-town or home-state based business networks which enable them to undercut their Hausa counterparts. The male Hausa provisions dealers do not appear to have been badly hit, since they can take their goods to Makarfi and other local centres on market days. Local women, however, who lack such freedom of movement, appear to be moving out of the provisions trade, except at the micro retail level.

One further activity in which profits appear to be improving is snack production, but only in the outlying hamlets. While their counterparts in the main village complained of high input costs and weak markets, Muslim Hausa women in some of the more distant hamlets claimed business was increasing. In the outlying hamlets, a large proportion of the inhabitants are non-Muslim Hausa or nomadic and semi-nomadic Fulani. The women in these two groups do not normally engage in snack production, but specialize in farming and the sale of milk products, respectively. While people from this area used to go into the village to buy prepared snacks, hard times and rising transport costs are diverting the market to more local producers within the hamlets. Once again, any significant improvement in local incomes is likely to undermine these new markets.

The information derived from the enterprise sample challenges many of the conventional assumptions concerning the non-farm sector. In Nasarawan Doya, the majority of non-farm activities operate all year round, rather than seasonally, show some potential for accumulation, and a significant level of integration with the wider regional, and even national economy, especially in the areas of trade and artisanal production. These discoveries do not, however, constitute grounds for a surge of optimism concerning the developmental potential of these activities. A combination of local structural constraints and the continuing pressures of structural adjustment, dramatically limit the economic potential of the non-farm sector. Low levels of education and skill formation, extremely limited access to capital and credit, and the intensifying squeeze in most activities between rising operating costs and weakening markets cast a pall over the income-generating potential of this sector. Furthermore, the positive association between the scale of agricultural production and success in the non-farm sector casts serious doubt on prospects for developing non-farm activities in order to compensate for pressures on agricultural incomes.

The overall picture that emerges from the enterprise sample is one of relatively limited and short-term accumulation potential at the top, and a mass of survival activities at the bottom, in which incomes are increasingly depressed by severe economic pressure in both the agricultural and the non-farm sectors. The few lucrative non-farm opportunities available are being seized largely by wealthy villagers or young entrepreneurs from southern Nigeria who move into the village from larger rural or urban centres. Contrary to the small rural towns thesis of non-farm enterprise expansion which sees successful enterprises moving up from villages to small towns (Baker & Pedersen 1992; Bryceson 1996), the prevailing direction of enterprise movement has been from the cities and towns down to the villages, driven predominantly by the saturation of the urban informal sector (Meagher 1999). Women's non-farm activities appear to be particularly disadvantaged by the current economic situation, owing to the combination of a relatively strict gender-division of labour with women's limited mobility, lack of participation in agriculture, and limited alternative sources of capital.

Plate 1
Motorcycle taxis waiting for passengers in the village square

Plate 2
Fulani women selling millet balls and sour milk (*fura da nono*)

Plate 3
Local sugar producers: the sugar crushing machine and horse

Plate 4
Local sugar producers: boiling and moulding the sugar

Plate 5
Girls selling snacks for their secluded mothers

Plate 6
A provisions shop in Nasarawan Doya

Plate 7
Local blacksmith's working hut

Plate 8
Local blacksmiths making hoe holders

6

Non-farm activities and
rural livelihood strategies

The analysis of non-farm activities from an enterprise perspective has focused on an assessment of the prospects of this sector as an alternative to agriculture within the context of structural adjustment. The enterprise perspective is useful as a means of indicating constraints and opportunities within the non-farm sector, the differential effects of these on different categories of enterprises, and as a means of capturing the role of migrants from outside the village community. However, owing to the purposive design of the enterprise sample, it tells us little about the relative importance of these activities in the village as a whole, and virtually nothing about the ways in which non-farm activities interact with agriculture in the context of individual and household-level livelihood strategies. In order to capture these very vital dimensions, we must return to the initial sample of village households to investigate the role of non-farm activities in wider structures of livelihood and accumulation.

Patterns of participation in non-farm activities
at the household level

From the household perspective, the most striking feature of non-farm participation in Nasarawan Doya is its extreme variability. Among household heads as well as dependents, men as well as women, participation in non-farm activities was found to vary according to season, economic circumstance, competing household demands, and shifts in the macro-economy. This, combined with the tendency to pursue multiple activities in certain seasons, made it extremely difficult to calculate participation rates for the various categories of non-farm activities. The percentage of household members indicating that they did not participate in any non-farm activity varied dramatically according to the season in which the question was asked. Furthermore, some household members might pursue three different activities in the same category, for example snack production, throughout the year, while others might have two or more different activities in different categories which they followed for only one season. In order to avoid any ambiguity, participation in a non-farm activity is, unless otherwise indicated, defined here as participation in any number of activities in a given category, at any point during the year under study. It should be kept in mind that the figures for non-farm participation include participation in agricultural wage labour.

Table 6.1 shows the participation rates in the various categories of non-farm activities for different categories of household members. These participation rates were obtained from the monitoring of economic activity throughout the year. Among men, the highest rate of non-farm participation was in agricultural wage labour, predominantly during the wet season. By many definitions this would not qualify as a non-farm activity at all, but, where non-farm is defined as 'non-own-farm', it remains the single most important source of income outside of household agriculture, particularly among male dependents. 30% of household heads, and 82% of male dependents, participated in this activity, making an overall male participation rate of 49%. The second most important activity among men was trade, dominated by household heads. Informal wage labour and agricultural processing were tied for third place. Both of these categories were dominated by local sugar production, with the wage labour aspect weighted heavily in favour of male dependents (44%), and the enterprise ownership weighted heavily in favour of household heads (37.5%).

Table 6.1
Non-farm participation among household members

Activity category	Men	Household heads	Women
Agricultural wage labour	49.2	30.0	0.0
Informal non-agricultural wage labour	23.8	12.5	1.5
Traditional crafts & load carrying	19.5	22.5	1.5
Traditional religion & medicine	1.6	2.5	0.0
Food & beverages	0.0	0.0	76.5
Agricultural processing	23.8	37.5	11.8
Trade	34.9	42.5	27.9
Clothing, hair & related services	1.6	0.0	1.5
Carpentry & modern building	0.0	0.0	0.0
Modern crafts & services	3.2	5.0	0.0
Transport	3.2	5.0	0.0
Asset rental	1.6	2.5	0.0
No non-farm activity	0.0	0.0	7.4
Total	162.4*	160.0*	128.1*

* Respondents may pursue more than one category of activity in the course of a year.
Source: Fieldwork 1996-97

Women's non-farm participation was heavily concentrated in food and beverage production, in which 76% of women participated, followed distantly by trade (28%), and even more distantly by agricultural processing (12%), which in the case of women refers essentially to manual crop threshing. Among women, trade was dominated by the micro-retailing of non-agricultural commodities (largely manufactured household necessities brought in from the rural towns and cities). By contrast, among male household members, participation in trade was dominated by agricultural commodities, both local (grain and livestock) and from southern Nigeria (oranges and kola).

The rates of non-participation in the non-farm sector were found to be extremely low, with no men and only 7.4% of women having no non-farm activities at any point in the year.[1] Owing to the fact that many respondents engage in two or even three different types of activities, the total of participation rates and non-participation rates is over 100%. On average, men engage in 1.6 different categories of activities in the course of a year, though many men also engaged in more than one activity of the same type. For example, those engaged in agricultural processing activities may combine local sugar production with the operation of a grain grinding machine, while traders may be involved in grain trading in one season and retailing of provisions in another. Although many women also engage in multiple activities, they average only 1.3 different types of activity per year, indicating a narrower range of activities, as well as a lower level of multiple engagements.

The data presented corroborates earlier indications of a sharp gender division of labour within the non-farm sector. What it does not show is the equally stark socio-economic division in access to particular non-farm activities. Among men, activities such as sugar production and modern crafts and services, which are comparatively lucrative as well as capital and skill intensive, are almost wholly dominated by operators in upper-stratum households. Conversely, activities such as agricultural and non-agricultural wage labour, and traditional crafts and load carrying, which have relatively few barriers to entry and comparatively low returns, are heavily biased in favour of lower-stratum households. Among women, the two major female activities – food and beverage production, and trade – showed a slight bias in favour of upper-stratum households, since access to any capital at all is a

---

[1]   It should be noted that the non-participation rate for household heads differs significantly from data obtained in the main sample, in which 12% of household heads indicted that they did not participate in any form of non-farm activity. The difference may arise from differences between the main and sub-samples (which seems unlikely given the random selection of the sub-sample), or from differences between what heads actually do relative to what they perceive themselves to be doing. In the main sample, heads were simply asked if they pursue any non-farm activities, while in the sub-sample, they were monitored on a seasonal basis.

major constraint on women's non-farm activities. The most capital intensive women's activities, found only in upper-stratum households, were speculative crop trading (included under trade) and tailoring. The only categories biased in favour of lower-stratum women were agricultural processing (involving only the sale of processing labour with minimal capital outlay), and no activity at all.

The seasonal variation in rates of participation in the non-farm economy is indicated in Table 6.2. In contrast with Table 6.1, the rates of non-participation are much higher when disaggregated seasonally. While all men participated in some form of non-farm activity at some point in the year, in any given season male non-participation ranged from 16% in the harvest season (the season traditionally devoted to non-farm activities), to 43% in the hot season. It should be noted that the season of lowest male participation in non-farm activities, the hot season, is also the season of least agricultural activity. It is in part because of the lack of agricultural activity that the hot season holds little in the way of male non-farm opportunities. It is outside the season of two of the mainstays of male non-farm involvement, agricultural wage labour and local sugar production, which are linked to the agricultural activities of cultivating and harvesting. Owing to a lack of capital, combined with the general absence of wage labouring opportunities, male dependents were particularly affected by the shortage of non-farm opportunities during the hot season. 78% of male dependents had no non-farm activity during this season, compared to only 22% of household heads, who have more capital to invest in various forms of self-employment less directly dependent on the agricultural cycle.

Disaggregating male participation, the period of greatest non-farm participation among household heads was in the harvest season (92% participation, or 8% non-participation), when rains cease, crops become available for trading, and villagers have some liquidity to be translated into non-farm capital and effective demand. Among male dependents, the period of greatest non-farm participation took place in the wet season (87% participation), if agricultural wage labour is included as non-farm, and during the harvest season (61% participation – largely as wage labour in sugar production), if agricultural wage labour is discounted. Among household heads, the rate of non-farm participation during the wet season, though not the highest, is still surprisingly high. 78% of household heads, and 81% of males overall, were engaged in non-farm activities during the wet season, the peak season for agricultural activity. Even if agricultural wage labour is removed from the calculations, 60% of household heads (though only 17% of male dependents) were found to participate in non-farm activities during the wet season. Whether agricultural wage labour is included or not, these findings raise questions about the extent to which economic change may have shifted non-farm activities from a position of seasonal complementarity with agriculture, to one of competition for agricultural labour time, particularly among households with limited access to hired labour.

Table 6.2
Seasonal participation (and non-participation) rates in non-farm activities among household members (% of category)

Season	Household heads	Male dependents	All men	Women
Wet	78 (22)	87 (13)	81 (19)	79 (21)
Harvest	92 (8)	70 (30)	84 (16)	69 (31)
Hot	78 (22)	22 (78)	57 (43)	57 (43)

Note: Figures in brackets represent non-participation rates.
Source: Fieldwork 1996-97

Among women, the highest non-farm participation rates occurred during the wet season, when 79% of women pursued some form of non-farm activity. This appears to relate to the expansion of the snack market during the agricultural season. As in the case of men, the hot season represented the season of lowest non-farm participation, with only 57% of women engaged in a non-farm activity.

The data on non-farm participation rates provides some indication that involvement in non-farm activities has increased over the past two decades, particularly among males. Data collected in the late 1960s and early 1970s by Norman and his colleagues in villages around Zaria, indicated that 25%

of household heads, and 5% of women had no non-farm activities (Norman et al. 1982; Simmons 1975). The data from Nasarawan Doya, which also lies within the wider hinterland of Zaria, suggests a significant increase in male non-farm participation, and a marginal decrease in female participation. However, the conclusiveness of these comparisons is limited by the extreme variation of non-farm participation in the course of the agricultural year, as well as by variations between perceived and actual levels of non-farm participation. Adult males, in particular, tend to under-represent their non-farm participation, owing to the perception of non-farm activities as peripheral and often incidental to men's main activity: farming. Because non-farm activities are more strongly associated with women than with men in rural Hausa Muslim culture, non-farm activities perceived as peripheral or conjunctural were, in some cases, dismissed as a sort of occupational 'noise' rather than a 'real' economic pursuit.[2] A sharper historical comparison would therefore require more information on the exact conditions under which the earlier data was obtained.

Further evidence suggesting an increase in male non-farm participation arises from the finding that, in Nasarawan Doya, 66% of household heads entered their current activities since the beginning of the structural adjustment period in 1986. This is in part an indication of increased recourse to non-farm sources of income, and in part an indication of a tendency of shift out of certain non-farm activities and into others, owing to changes in the profitability or affordability of various activities under structural adjustment. This process has tended to reinforce the non-farm income differentiation between households in the lower and upper strata. Members of lower-stratum households routinely lack the resources to make timely shifts in activities in response to changing opportunities, and are more constrained to shift into relatively low-cost, low-return activities when they do make a change.

---

[2] This is illustrated by the difference between non-farm participation rates obtained from the once-off household questionnaire, and the participation levels found through regular monitoring. While only 88% of household heads recognized themselves as participating in non-farm activities, 100% of males actually did (or 95% if agricultural wage labour is excluded from the calculations).

A look at the locations of the activities abandoned in the process of shifting into currently held activities suggests that non-farm activities have also become more locally based than was the case before the structural adjustment period. 39% of the activities abandoned were in locations outside of Nasarawan Doya, including almost 20% carried out in the Lagos/Ibadan area. Many of these were trading activities, abandoned because of the rising cost of goods and transport. By contrast, the survey of currently held activities found that only 15% of household heads practised non-farm activities outside Nasarawan Doya and the outlying hamlets. Only 6%, mostly traders, practised their activities in the nearby agricultural bulking markets of Sundu and Makarfi, and a mere 7% in Lagos/Ibadan. Although participation in non-farm activities appears to be increasing among male villagers, the geographical scope of these activities appears to be narrowing, concentrating a growing number of activities within increasingly local, and economically weakened, markets. It should be noted that the bulk of these changes involve failing long-distance traders rather than migrants, and, as will be demonstrated subsequently, does not indicate a high level of return migration, nor any significant return flow of skills or capital into the village.

Non-farm livelihood strategies

Investigating the structure of participation by household members in various non-farm activities generates useful information about the relative importance of particular categories of non-farm activity. However, in order to appreciate the role played by non-farm activities in *household*, rather than individual, livelihood strategies, it is necessary to look at the non-farm profiles of entire households, rather than surveying levels of participation of individuals in various categories of activities. Household non-farm profiles more effectively illustrate the extent to which the role of non-farm incomes in household livelihood strategies is influenced by the command of capital and skills at the household level, rather than simply by individual characteristics influencing access.

The first profile is of the poorest household in the sample. This household has four members, but only two are economically active. The household head is 70 years old. He does wet season, but no dry season, farming, and has only Koranic education. He has only one non-farm activity, which is to carry loads with his donkey. He also used to do small-scale trade, but had to abandon this activity in 1989 owing to a lack of capital. The head's one wife makes bean cakes only in the dry season. She abandoned the production of breakfast porridge in 1993 because she was not getting any profit. Both the head and his wife receive a substantial portion of their household income in the form gifts of money and clothing from rural relatives.

The second household is one of the richest households in the sample. This household has six economically active members. The head, who is a young man of 25, has Western primary school education, and engages in wet and dry season farming. He also engages in local sugar production, trades in engine oil, and has a motorcycle and grinding machine that he uses for commercial purposes. He used to engage in wholesale crop trading, but shifted to sugar production in 1991 because he felt it was more profitable. The first wife of the household head trades in washing detergent, millet and groundnuts throughout the year. The second wife trades in cooked beans as well as tigernuts (*aya*), a local snack, for two of the three seasons of the year. She abandoned the production of bean cakes in 1996 because her daughter, who served as her sales agent, got married. The eldest of three economically active male dependents in the household farms and engages in casual labour during the harvest season. The second male dependent is a farmer and tailor, and practises his trade in the wet as well as the dry season. The third male dependent engages in agricultural wage labour during the wet season, sugar labour during the harvest season, and does brick making in the dry season, all in addition to farming.

These profiles suggest that the critical question of non-farm accumulation does not just revolve around the ability of individuals to participate in the more lucrative types of activities. It also concerns the ability of individual household members to engage in multiple activities, and the ability of households to maximize the participation of other household members in additional, preferably lucrative, forms of income generation. In better-off households, heads tend to use their superior resource position to contribute to the capital and skill base of wives and economically active dependents, which encourages a more collective, household-centred livelihood strategy. In poorer households, the weaker resource position of the head tends to have a more centripetal effect, throwing wives and dependents toward alternative networks of assistance, or more individualized livelihood strategies (Wallace 1978; Ross 1987). These differentiated patterns of household and individual livelihood strategies will be explored in more detail below.

The importance of non-farm activities in total labour time

It is clear from the evidence presented so far that non-farm activities play an important role in both individual and household livelihood strategies, but this still leaves open the question of the importance of non-farm activities relative to agriculture. Measuring the importance of non-farm activities requires an examination of their relative share in the labour time and incomes of household members.

An assessment of the share of non-farm activities in total labour time was based on a seasonal monitoring of the number of hours spent per week on personal and household agriculture, agricultural wage labour, other non-farm activities, and domestic work. The regular timing of the five muslim prayers was used to assist respondents in assessing how long they spent on the various categories of activities. The share of non-farm activities in total labour time involves the total of the time spent in agricultural wage labour and in other non-farm activities, as a percentage of the total time spent in all of the activities mentioned above.

Non-farm activities were found to account for an average of 36.3% of total working hours in the course of a year. Disaggregated by gender, non-farm activities represented 27% of women's total working time, and 46% of men's working time (Table 6.3). Further disaggregating the data on male household members, heads were found to spend an average of 53% of their time on non-farm activities, by far the largest share of any other category of household member. This is a surprising finding, given that household heads also have primary responsibility for household agriculture. However, the demands of agriculture appear to constrain heads' (and male) work time generally, only during the wet season. During this season, while household and own-account agriculture occupied 72% of heads' (and overall male) working time, non-farm work consumed 27% of male working time, and domestic work accounted for the remaining 1%. The share of male non-farm work rose markedly in the remaining two seasons, especially among heads, given their greater access to capital to fund non-farm activities off season. Among women, seasonal variations in non-farm work time were comparatively minor, owing to the relative lack of participation in agriculture. Domestic labour was the major competitor for women's work time, occupying an average of 72% of women's work time across all seasons, while agriculture accounted for less than 1%.

Table 6.3
Time spent on agricultural and non-farm activities as a share of total working time (%)

Household members	Wet season	Harvest season	Hot season	Annual average
Agriculture				
Men	72.4	23,1	16,6	41.5
Heads of household	71.7	17.9	5.6	42.2
Women	1.3	0.0	0.4	0.7
Non-farm activities				
Men	26.6	76.3	56.8	45.6
Heads of household	26.8	81.3	78.4	52.7
Women	29.0	30.6	21.9	27.2

Source: Fieldwork 1996-97

The share of non-farm activities in working time showed some variation by socio-economic stratum, though the direction of change varied according to gender. Upper-stratum women spent a slightly larger share of their time (29.2%) on non-farm activities than lower-stratum women (24.3%), while upper-stratum men spent a slightly smaller share of their time

(44.2%) on non-farm pursuits than lower-stratum men (47.7%). This reflects the greater ability of men to hire labour when they intensify involvement in non-farm activities, while better-off women tend to intensify involvement in income-generating activities by shedding domestic chores onto junior women.

An examination of recent trends in time use indicates that women not only spend a lower overall share of their time on non-farm activities than men, they have reduced the amount of time they spend on non-farm activities since the early 1990s. The majority of women indicated they spend less time on non-farm activities now than they did five years ago. By contrast, the majority of men indicated they now spend more time on non-farm activities.

Women's non-farm involvement does not appear to have been constrained by increasing domestic demands, as a majority of women also indicated that they now spend less time on domestic work as well. The reduction in domestic work time appears to be largely a life cycle issue, as children grow and, in some cases, new wives enter the household. However, the reduction in time spent on non-farm activities is connected with wider economic pressures. Women claimed that their involvement in non-farm activities had declined owing to a lack of capital and declining markets for their activities. Most women lacked the capital to shift into more profitable women's activities, such as speculative crop trading, and generally felt that the profitability of women's non-farm activities had declined since the early 1990s, owing to a lack of effective demand. The extremely narrow range of acceptable women's activities also limits their access to new opportunities. In addition to the general decline in profitability of their activities, women's capital was being further eroded by the rising cost of gifts for ceremonies, and, in many cases, increased economic demands for household provisioning.

In the case of men, rising involvement in non-farm activities does not appear to have been at the expense of their own farming activities. Barely one-quarter of men indicated they spent less time on farming, while over 40% said they now spend more time on farming. In contrast to women, men claimed that non-farm activities remained relatively profitable, although the additional income did not always keep up with the rising cost of living and farming. Perhaps more important in encouraging increased male involvement in non-farm activities was their stabilizing effect on seasonal income levels, and the continued pressure of rising household and farming costs. In contrast to women, whose capital base was being eroded by these pressures, men's superior access to capital and greater occupational flexibility allowed them to respond to a similar set of pressures by increasing their involvement in non-farm activities.

Overall, the time-use data indicates that non-farm activities play a central – and increasing – role in male livelihood strategies. Despite the fact that men have virtually sole responsibility for farming activities, non-farm activities account for nearly half of their working time. Moreover, men felt that the share of non-farm activities in their working time had increased over the last five years. Women, despite being largely excluded from direct involvement in agriculture, spend less than one-third of their working time on non-farm activities, and even this level of involvement has been declining. An assessment of the implications of these countervailing trends for the overall economic role of non-farm activities requires a consideration of the weight of non-farm incomes in total household incomes.

Non-farm incomes as a share of household incomes

Evidence of a significant reliance on non-farm sources of income was borne out by data collected on the main sources of household income in Nasarawan Doya. Gross household incomes were calculated on the basis of information collected on income from sold and unsold crops, sales of livestock and livestock products, non-farm activities and gifts. Owing to difficulties associated with the collection of precise income data in this context, the data on income in all categories represent gross takings, rather than income net of production costs. Table 6.4 shows the relative importance of these various income categories. In order to provide a more comprehensive picture of the relative importance of non-farm incomes, they were calculated as a share of household cash income, and also as a share of the total value of cash income and unsold agricultural produce.

Table 6.4
Relative shares of household income sources

Stratum	% gifts of total cash income	% live stock of tot. cash income	% crop sales of total cash income	% NFA of total cash income	% NFA of total cash & produce income	% Agric. wage labour of total cash income*	% Agric. wage labour of total cash & produce income*
Upper	0.6	4.2	25.0	70.2	60.8	2.2	1.8
Lower	0.4	4.7	20.9	74.0	60.2	6.3	3.9
Sample avg.	0.6	4.4	23.4	71.6	60.6	4.1	2.8

* The agricultural wage labour income share is presented as a sub-component of the non-farm income share.
Source: Fieldwork 1996-97

The data indicates that, at the household level, non-farm income sources account for 72% of total cash incomes, and 61% of total cash and produce incomes. Surprisingly, there is comparatively little variation among household economic strata, although non-farm income shares are slightly higher as a share of cash income among lower-stratum households. Disaggregating the data by gender and household position reveals that, among household heads, non-farm incomes account for an average of 54% of total individual cash income; among women, they account for 78% of total individual cash incomes, and among male dependents, about 50% of total cash incomes, with comparatively little variation among socio-economic strata.

Income from agricultural wage labour, presented here as a sub-component of the non-farm income share, accounts for a surprisingly small proportion of non-farm earnings given the extent of participation in this activity. Agricultural wage labour accounts for an average of only 4% of household cash income, and just under 3% of total cash and produce income. Among lower stratum households, the importance of this income source was slightly higher, at 6% of cash incomes, and 4% of total cash and produce incomes. This very low share derives partially from the lack of importance of wage labour in women's incomes, but rests even more significantly on its comparative lack of importance in the non-farm incomes of household heads.[3] This testifies to the continued priority of the house-hold farm in local livelihood strategies. Except in cases of extreme eco-nomic pressure, household heads still give priority to the needs of the household farm, and concentrate on non-farm sources of income that compete less directly for their labour at critical times. Even in the wet season, many non-farm activities are pursued in the late afternoon and evening, after men have returned from working on the farm. Only male dependents showed a significant dependence on agricultural wage labour, which accounted, on average, for nearly half of their non-farm incomes.

While this may appear to confirm claims regarding the limited develop-ment of agricultural wage labour markets in rural Africa, that assessment would be misleading. Quite the contrary, the Nigerian savanna is charac-terized by an extremely high level of agricultural wage labour use and well-developed wage labour markets. Although the above findings on income sources make it clear that local households provide a very limited amount of wage labour to each other, it says nothing about the extent of other sources of agricultural labour. As indicated at the beginning of the study, the main sources of agricultural wage labour in this area come from outside the village, largely from the drier regions to the north, while labour from the southern part of the state comes into the village in the off-season to work on dry season farms. The limited importance of agricultural wage labour in local incomes should not be equated with a limited importance of agricultural wage labour in the local farming system.

Further disaggregating the data on income shares yields a number of interesting insights into the role of non-farm incomes in the determination of household income. First of all, the data on income shares corroborate the time-share data on the importance of non-farm sources of income in male livelihood strategies, even during the wet season. The findings indicate that household heads earned an average of 38% of their annual non-farm earnings during the wet season, while male dependents earned 51% of their

---

[3] Although agricultural wage labour was of very minor importance to household incomes on average, it should be noted that in 10% of the sample households, this income source accounted for over 10% of cash income, and for 45% of cash income in one household.

non-farm incomes during the wet season. In the case of male dependents, this seasonal bias reflects the importance of agricultural wage-labour in non-farm incomes. In the case of household heads, however, it reflects the pressing expenditure needs of the wet season, when marketable crops are exhausted, household food supplies may be running low, and cash is needed to pay for fertilizer and agricultural labour. While this indicates an economic complementarity between agriculture and the non-farm sector in terms of income flows, it suggests that any expansion of non-farm partici- pation may pose problems of competition for labour time, both in the time budgets of household heads, and in terms of heads' access to the agricul- tural labour time of their male dependents.

A second illuminating finding is that the incomes of lower-stratum women were found to contribute more to total household income, both pro- portionately and absolutely, than the incomes of upper-stratum women. In lower-stratum households, women's incomes, which are predominantly non-farm, contributed 17% to household cash income, compared to only 13% in upper-stratum households. This evidence appears to corroborate the findings of Hill (1977) and Matlon (1978) that women's predominantly non-farm incomes tend to moderate, rather than accentuate, rural income inequality. However, three important qualifications should be noted. First, the differential in the share of household cash income contributed by lower and upper-stratum women is fairly slight – only 4%. Secondly, differences in non-farm income levels do not account for the whole of the differential between the total incomes of lower-stratum and upper-stratum women. 40% of this income differential is accounted for by gifts and sales of livestock. Finally, evidence of increasing pressure on women's incomes, particularly in lower-stratum households, suggests that any moderating im- pact they may have on household income inequality is being eroded in the face of current economic pressures.

To summarize the findings so far, there is clear evidence that non-farm incomes play a critical role in household incomes among both poorer as well as better-off households, significantly outweighing agricultural pro- duction in their contribution to household livelihoods. Evidence cited earlier indicates that, while female involvement in non-farm activities is under increasing economic pressure, male involvement in non-farm activities has increased. In fact, in Nasarawan Doya, men perceive themselves to be more dependent on non-farm activities than in the past. In interviews, men indicated that this increase in dependence was motivated, not by the rising profitability of non-farm activities, but by the declining profitability of agriculture. There was a general consensus among the majority of household members, both male and female, that real incomes from most non-farm activities have declined. The high cost of inputs and equipment, combined with weak markets were seen to have eroded the income potential of many of these activities. Those from better-off households maintained that some activities were more profitable now if one had the money to enter them. On the whole, however, it was felt that non-farm activities generated less in the way of real income than they had in the past.

One might conclude from this that, at least among the lower stratum of households, the economic preponderance of non-farm incomes in household livelihood strategies is more by default than by design – what could be characterized as all 'push' and no 'pull'. Rising agricultural production costs, combined with the rising cost of living, have made both household survival and continued participation in agriculture increasingly dependent on access to non-farm income. Among the upper stratum of households, the emergence of new non-farm opportunities has provided new avenues for accumulation, though not so much as an alternative to, as in conjunction with, agriculture.

Non-farm activities and agriculture:
Investment patterns and occupational identities

Examining the importance of non-farm incomes as a share of working time and of household income provides a useful indicator of the considerable economic significance of the non-farm sector. However, it tends to create a rather binary image of agriculture vs. non-farm pursuits, in terms of individual labour time, access to household labour, levels of profitability and income streams. This raises the spectre of competition rather than complementarity, particularly in view of evidence of high levels of non-farm activity during the principal agricultural season. While the issue of competition should be taken seriously, it also tends to mask the significant degree of economic interdependence that continues to exist between the two sectors.

An economic orientation that emphasizes the economic interdependence of agriculture and the non-farm sector, rather than economic competition between the two, is evident in the economic rationale of men's investment patterns, and the overall influence of current economic change on the formation of men's occupational identities. For obvious reasons, the economic relationship between agriculture and the non-farm sector is much less central to women's investment and occupational strategies. Owing to differences in economic priorities and occupational opportunities, particularly influenced by their lack of involvement in agriculture, women display very different investment patterns, which will be considered in the subsequent section dealing with household welfare and social networks.

An analysis of men's investment patterns between sectors makes it clear that increased dependence on non-farm activities has not eroded the strong interdependence between non-farm and agricultural sources of income. When asked to indicate the sources of capital for investment in non-farm activities, crop sales were identified as the primary source by the majority of both household heads and male dependents. The dependence on agriculture for non-farm capital was particularly high among upper-stratum heads. By contrast, one-third of lower-stratum heads had to turn to the non-farm sector for capital to engage in non-farm activities (e.g. wage labouring to get capital for petty trade), owing to their more limited ability to produce an agricultural surplus above household consumption and basic cash needs.

Non-farm activities had a much more limited role as a source of capital for re-investment in agriculture. Three-quarters of household heads indicated that the primary use of their non-farm earnings was for maintaining the household, while less than one-third of household heads indicated that they used their non-farm earnings for agricultural investment. While immediate household needs significantly constrained the ability of household heads to invest non-farm earnings in agriculture, non-farm incomes still figured second to crop sales as a source of resources for agricultural investment. Among upper-stratum households, non-farm activities figured as the most important source of capital for both land and input purchases, owing to the ability of upper-stratum males to pursue much more lucrative types of non-farm activity.

Given this symbiotic relationship between agricultural and non-farm incomes, the increasingly central role of non-farm activities in male livelihood strategies has not triggered any discernible shift in occupational identities in Nasarawan Doya. 99% of the household heads, and 100% of male dependents defined their primary occupation as farming. Perhaps more revealing, only 45% of household heads indicated in initial interviews that they had any secondary occupations, despite the fact that all of them were found to pursue some form of non-farm activity, and that non-farm activities occupied on average over 50% of their working time and generated roughly 60% of household income in cash and kind. In fact, an interview held with a group of men concerning the growing importance of non-farm activities broke into a debate concerning whether men have non-farm activities at all. It was argued by some present that non-farm activities are the preserve of women, and men are just farmers. Non-farm activities are largely perceived, not as occupational alternatives to farming, but as a means men employ to remain farmers, and where possible, to accumulate additional resources, some of which will be devoted to agricultural expansion. One villager later summed up the situation with a Hausa saying: if the drumming changes, the dance also changes. Farmers adapt to the changing economic times, but that does not change what they are.

The strong attachment to agricultural identities despite high levels of economic dependence on non-farm activities should come as no surprise. Various studies have pointed to the resilience of agricultural identities despite increasing dependence on non-farm sources of livelihood among the rural poor (Williams 1988; Lennihan 1987). Whether the process was cast as diversification or proletarianization, the result was a continued attachment to agriculture both as an activity and as a central feature of occupational identity, even in the face of high levels of dependence on other sources of income. In the 1990s, however, with the contraction of wage labouring opportunities both in the rural and in the urban areas, the central theoretical question regarding the fate of the poor is no longer one of proletarianization but of survival. The continued commitment of male household members to agricultural identities tends to mask the increasing difficulty with which some households reproduce themselves not only as farming units, but as physical beings, even with recourse to non-farm activities.

Migration patterns and non-farm options

Little is said in the current non-farm literature about the role of regional, as opposed to household-level, migration patterns in shaping the development of the non-farm sector. This relates not only to the outward or return migration of locals, but also to the in-migration of non-locals from other parts of the savanna, or from other parts of the country and beyond. In Nasarawan Doya, four main trends are evident in migration patterns under structural adjustment. These are in-migration from other parts of the guinea and sahel savanna, in-migration from southern Nigeria, return migration from locals, and, although structural adjustment lore tells us to expect otherwise, rural-urban out-migration. The overall impact of these migration patterns has been to produce a narrowing rather than an expansion of non-farm opportunities for local inhabitants.

Although largely ignored by the rural-urban bias of the non-farm literature, circulatory rural-rural migration constitutes the major migratory trend in the savanna area. In the grain surplus region, in-migration from less favoured parts of the savanna has been the characteristic feature of migration patterns for decades. The migrants involved in this pattern of migration are largely Koranic students and agricultural labourers, as well as itinerant practitioners of low-income non-farm activities as indicated in the enterprise sample. With regard to in-migrants, 30% of households in the household sample reported having migrants living with them, and the majority of these migrants were Koranic students. 42% of households reported having migrants working for them, all of whom were agricultural wage labourers from other parts of the savanna. Predictably, the upper stratum of households had the highest percentage of migrants working for them. Both types of in-migrants tend to operate seasonally; they come on an annual basis for three to four months.

In-migration from southern Nigeria, although the most politically and economically visible, represents the smallest migratory trend, accounting for less than 1% of population movements in the village. However, it functions to cream off some of the more lucrative non-farm opportunities. While the in-migration of southern Nigerians does serve to bring skills and capital into the village, the extent to which these assets contribute to local entrepreneurial and economic development is limited by institutional and cultural barriers. The apprenticeship, credit and supply networks that account for the success of this group are, as previously mentioned, organized on an ethnic/hometown basis, rather than integrating with local economic or occupational institutions. On the whole, the economic activities of this group tend to channel incomes and investment away from resident households and local agriculture. Thus the dominant patterns of in-migration are low-skilled and seasonal, while the better-endowed category of in-migrants is both small and economically dis-integrated from the rest of the population.

Patterns of out-migration show a similar picture of largely seasonal movements, and very limited potential for stimulating inflows of skills and capital. 25% of households in the sub-sample had out-migrants, the majority of whom were junior males. Two-thirds of this out-migration was temporary, and one-third was permanent. One-third of the out-migrants were Koranic students, one-third were traders, and only one-fifth were civil servants, though the latter were all from upper-stratum households. 75% of the out-migration was initiated since the onset of adjustment, including that of civil servants, which is likely a reflection of new local opportunities for public employment generated by the creation of Makarfi Local Government in 1991.

Another significant trend in local migration patterns involves a trend toward return migration from the urban back to the rural areas. One quarter of households in the sub-sample reported having return migrants, and all but one of the returns occurred since the onset of structural adjustment. However, this process does not appear to be bringing skills and capital back into the community to fuel the growth of the non-farm sector. On the contrary, return migration has involved a retreat from collapsed opportunities outside rather than a repatriation of entrepreneurial resources. More than half of the returnees were returning Koranic students, and one-third were traders who had run out of capital. 85% of the returnees had no formal education, and two-thirds of returnees have taken up no activity other than farming since their return. The better-educated and skilled migrants, concentrated overwhelmingly in the upper stratum of households, have tended not to return. It is also worth noting that the number of return migrants since 1986 equals the number of out-migrants over the same period, which would tend to support macro-economic evidence that, under adjustment, there is no net trend toward return migration in Nigeria (Dike 1994).

What emerges from this investigation of household livelihood strategies is that non-farm activities have come to play a major role in household income-generation as well as household labour time. Despite their surprising economic importance, even during the growing season, non-farm activities remain complementary with agriculture, and have tended to reinforce rather than undermine both agricultural activity and male agricultural identities. There are, however, important signs of strain within the non-farm sector. The non-farm incomes of women and lower-stratum households appear to be under increasing pressure in the face of rising production costs, declining access to capital, and weakening effective demand, confirming similar findings in the enterprise sample. Moreover, the contraction of the urban economy has tended to reduce inflows of capital to village households, without bringing any significant return flow of skills. The only skilled in-migration involves migrants from southern Nigeria, who, for the most part, come without their families and redirect investment to their home areas. While better-off households have been able to use their superior resource position to seize new opportunities and maximize household incomes through a combination of agricultural and non-farm activities, the majority of local households have succumbed to coping strategies in which the combination of agricultural and non-farm activities are dictated by economic pressures beyond their control. Within this context, the ability of the non-farm sector to support what remains an agriculturally-based material and moral economy is at best questionable.

7

Household welfare
and social networks:
A non-farm perspective

An assessment of the impact of non-farm activities on household welfare requires more than a simple assessment of their importance as a source of additional household income. Just as the role of non-farm activities in rural development is mediated through their relationship with agriculture, so their implications for household welfare are mediated through the structure of economic relations within the household, as well as relations between households. In the context of structural adjustment, the traditional division of economic responsibilities between men and women has come under increasing pressure, which has limited, and in some cases undermined, the potentially beneficial role of non-farm activities on household welfare, particularly among poor households. Women's non-farm incomes have been particularly affected by these pressures. In the face of intensifying economic pressures on rural households, women's economic responsibilities within the household have tended to increase, despite a context of declining real incomes in women's activities.

Economic pressures on individual incomes and household welfare have tended to highlight the importance of ties of mutual assistance linking rural households and their members to wider networks based on kinship or community. In the rural areas, however, such networks have often been enfeebled, rather than strengthened, by the pressures of economic restructuring, severely limiting their capacity to render assistance. In some cases, assistance through social networks may galvanize the economic efforts of household members into a predominantly household-centred economic strategy. In other cases, particularly where the household head is unable (even with the external assistance available to him) to meet the economic needs of household members, external networks may become the focus of alternative economic strategies that draw the resources of household members away from the household.

Household welfare and responsibilities for household provisioning

Despite the major contribution of non-farm activities to the incomes of upper as well as lower-stratum households, the majority of households in Nasarawan Doya appeared to be under considerable economic pressure. There was evidence of a substantial reduction in access to a range of basic household goods, including food and clothing. Over half of the households in the sub-sample reported cutting back, relative to the early 1990s, on local 'luxuries', such as tea, bread and eggs. Despite already low levels of protein in the local diet, in which the average rural household ate meat only a few times in a month, approximately 40% of households overall, and over 50% of lower-stratum households, had cut back on purchases of meat relative to the early 1990s. Only 4% of households reported an increase in their consumption of meat over the same period.

These 'cutbacks' are indicative of a situation in which an increasing number of household heads were unable to meet their basic economic responsibilities for household provisioning. According to the Islamic norms that govern allocation of household responsibilities among the Muslim

Hausa, the provisioning of the household is a male responsibility. This refers to all basic household necessities, including basic clothing, fuel and items required for the preparation of household meals, right down to the money for grinding the staple grain and the matches for lighting the cooking fire. Women's incomes are reserved for 'personal' use, meaning expenditure on their own relatives, gifts for ceremonies, and extra expenditures for themselves and their children (Imam 1993; Jackson 1984).

In the face of mounting economic pressure, and in direct contravention of local Islamic norms, there has been a tendency for men to transfer a growing share of the burden of household maintenance onto their wives. 39% of wives indicated that they were often responsible for the purchase of various ingredients for household meals, such as salt, oil, and seasonings, as well as the cost of grinding grain and the purchase of kerosine for cooking or lighting. 46% indicated increased economic responsibility for the purchase of children's clothing, 54% for the purchase of their own basic clothing, and 86% of women indicated they had been left with growing responsibility for the purchase of laundry soap and basic toiletries. Traditionally, women have granted such assistance to their husbands in the form of short-term credit (Watts 1983). In the face of the skyrocketing cost of living, however, some women in Nasarawan Doya maintained that there was little point in granting credit for household necessities, since husbands were unable to repay it. Contributions made by women to the running of the household were increasingly, implicitly or explicitly, regarded as gifts.

These trends are neither isolated nor recent. Research conducted in the late 1980s and early 1990s in nearby Hausa villages and in traditional urban quarters found these tendencies already developing (Meagher & Yunusa 1996; Imam 1993). Within the framework of Islamic ideology, however, the increased economic responsibility of women for household provisioning continues to be portrayed only as a form of 'help' or 'pitching in', casting as a voluntary and intermittent something that is increasingly becoming the norm.

While the additional economic burdens borne by women sound comparatively minor, their weight must be evaluated in the context of the comparatively restricted opportunities for income-generation among secluded rural women, and the low level of their capital base and incomes. The average weekly profit of women in the household sub-sample was N47 (US$ 0.55), at a time when a 0.75l bottle of groundnut oil cost N60, and a bar of cheap laundry soap was over N20. As households have become more dependent on the resources of women's non-farm activities, the necessity of contributing resources to the task of basic household maintenance had begun to weaken the viability of these activities. Nearly two-thirds of the wives in the sample indicated that their non-farm capital was being eroded by the need to help their husbands with basic household provisioning.

Increased household demands on women's resources, combined with the low level of women's non-farm incomes and the narrow range of acceptable income-generating activities, has tended to undermine the viability of women's non-farm activities. As one woman noted, women had less capital and markets were weaker, but one had to do something to bring in money, even engaging in activities with extremely low returns. In interviews, women maintained that, while economic pressures drove them to look for more non-farm activities to do, lack of capital had created a situation in which they engaged in fewer activities than they used to. Thus, the majority of women found themselves in a situation in which economic pressures within the household both encouraged them to pursue non-farm activities and limited their ability to do so.

Sources of women's non-farm capital

The evidence presented above points to a significant erosion and realignment of women's traditional sources of capital. Traditionally, capital for women's non-farm activities is provided by their husbands, though women could bring into marriage income-generating assets provided by their parents. In addition, women often invested accumulated resources in small stock, particularly goats and sheep, which were kept as a form of saving, and sold to meet expenses, such as additional capital requirements for their non-farm activities, or credit requests from household members (Simmons 1990; Watts 1983). Gifts received in the context of festivals and ceremonies were also important sources of resources, but traditionally functioned as only one of a range of alternative sources.

In the context of adjustment, many of these sources of capital are drying up. Husbands are increasingly unable to meet basic household needs, let alone their obligations for the provision of capital for their wives' income-generating activities. At the same time, rearing livestock appears to have become increasingly impracticable for women as a savings strategy. The rising cost of small stock relative to women's incomes, combined with the rising cost of medicine in the event of illness, and declining access to household labour to provide feed, have all made small stock increasingly unaffordable as well as risky. In Nasarawan Doya, women's livestock holdings were found to be extremely low, averaging 1.2 small stock among upper-stratum women, and 1.5 among lower-stratum women. Income from sales of small stock constituted a negligible proportion of women's incomes, and was almost never cited as an important source of capital or of household credit. Although livestock have become significantly less important as a source of capital, it was noted that lower-stratum women earned nearly twice the income of upper-stratum women from the sale of small stock, testifying to the more intense economic pressures on lower-stratum women. As mentioned above, higher incomes earned from the sale of small stock accounted for a significant proportion of the differential between the incomes of upper-stratum and lower-stratum women.

The result of the narrowing of women's sources of capital has been an increasing concentration of women's dependence on assistance from relatives. In the household sample as well as the enterprise sample, 'gifts from relatives' was cited by women as the main source of capital for non-farm activities. Although the data presented above on the relative contributions of various sources to household income (Table 6.4) indicates that the contribution of gifts is negligible, the data tends to mask the importance of gifts in women's (as opposed to household) incomes for a number of reasons. First of all, gifts are the only income source that does not involve any production costs (unless one were to take into account the costs of maintaining social relations with those who contribute gifts), with the result that they appear less significant when included alongside gross income categories. Secondly, the category of gifts as a proportion of income only included cash gifts, while a significant proportion of gifts, especially to upper-stratum women, were received in kind, particularly in the form of grain and cloth.[1] Finally, the household data obscures differences in the importance of gifts in women's relative to men's incomes, since women contributed only a small share of total household income, but received the bulk of the gift income.

When the data on gifts is disaggregated, it can be seen that women's income from gifts was higher than that of men both in absolute terms and as a proportion of their total income. If grain as well as cash is taken into account (but not cloth or clothing), women received an average of N465 in gifts, while men received an average of N310. Given the wide discrepancy in male and female incomes, gifts were clearly much more significant as a share of female incomes. Efforts made to obtain data on non-farm *profit* levels, rather than turnover, showed that gifts of cash and grain alone accounted for over 15% of women's net cash incomes, while the share of gifts in men's net cash incomes was on the order of 2%.

Not only did gifts account for an important share of women's net incomes, they played a critical role in non-farm capital. Over 60% of wives of household heads indicated that the major use of financial assistance from relatives, which was indicated to come largely in the form of gifts rather than loans, was non-farm capital. The next most important use was clothing, an option selected by only 20% of upper-stratum women, but 45% of lower-stratum women. This reflects the greater tendency for upper-stratum women to receive gifts of clothing in kind, while the relatives of lower-stratum women were less able to afford such bulk expenditures. These patterns reflect both a narrowing of women's access to capital and economic assistance, and a concomitant shift in economic strategies from husbands and household-centred strategies, to a greater reliance on networks of natal kin.

---

[1] Valuing gifts received in kind requires extremely detailed information, which proved excessively time-consuming to collect given the broader aims of the research. Gifts were usually specified in generic terms, i.e. cloth or wrappers, which may vary in value from N900 to over N5,000 depending on the type of cloth. Assessing the value in each case would have entailed additional questions on the quantity and the type or brand of cloth, which was often met with claims of being unable to recall.

This economic decentralization is predominantly a strategy of lower-stratum women.

Women's investment priorities

Among women, whose identities and activity patterns are much less directly bound up with agriculture, investment patterns of non-farm incomes were found to be very different from those of men. As in the case of men, however, women's priorities for the investment of non-farm income reflected a concern for maintaining and expanding the source of non-farm capital, as well as for meeting basic needs. Agriculture played a negligible role in this process, given the constraints on women's own account farming, and the declining ability of husbands to provide women with non-farm capital. As noted above, gifts from outside the household, rather than crop sales from within it were found to constitute the main source of non-farm capital. The main source of these gifts was from male natal kin. It is well to keep in mind that the ultimate source of such gifts is undoubtedly closely bound up with crop sales of male relatives or produce given in kind, once again underlining the ultimate dependence of even women's non-farm activities on agriculture, albeit on production units outside the household.

This preamble represents an attempt to situate the economic logic of women's non-farm expenditure patterns. While men devoted the bulk of their non-farm earnings to household maintenance and agriculture, the two most important areas of expenditure for women's non-farm incomes were ceremony gifts and the purchase and accumulation of dowry goods for the eventual marriage of their daughters. Averaged across the three agricultural seasons, just under 50% of women identified ceremonies as a major use of non-farm profits, followed by dowry goods, which were a priority for an average of 20% of women. Household goods and expenditure on children came third in the order of investment priorities, and re-investment in non-farm activities was barely mentioned at all. What initially appears to be frivolous or economically irrational consumption expenditure takes on a certain economic sense when viewed in the light of the social mechanisms through which women gain access to capital, as well as mechanisms for maintaining access to sources of economic security in times of trouble.

As indicated above, gifts from relatives, predominantly male natal kin described as 'brothers', represented the major source of non-farm capital for a majority of women in the study, as well as constituting an important source of assistance for meeting basic consumption needs. And exchange of gifts between relatives is done largely in the context of ceremonies. Thus, expenditure on ceremony attendance and ceremony gifts represents a means of reinforcing social relations with natal kin, and the economic claims embedded in those social relations. Similar strategies of maintaining economic claims on male natal kin were earlier referred to with regard to land inheritance among rural Hausa women in Kano State (Ross 1987). Expenditure on dowry goods relates to the constitution of a capital base for daughters to take with them into marriage, and hence has implications for the income-generating options of the next generation of women. This is not to pretend that the economic decisions of Hausa women are determined wholly by rational calculation, or that cultural considerations related to obligations, status and custom do not heavily influence women's expenditure decisions. It is simply to point out that women's expenditure choices, however culturally determined, are not economically irrational, and tend to reinforce, rather than to dissipate, women's access to resources for investment in non-farm activities.

Social networks and community associations

The preceding discussion of women's reliance on social and economic ties with natal kin illustrates one of the ways in which the pressures of structural adjustment on household welfare have tended to increase the importance of inter-household networks and associations. Various studies have highlighted the importance of social networks and community groups in coping with the economic pressures of adjustment (Berry 1993b; Bratton 1989; Meagher and Mustapha 1997; Jamal & Weeks 1993). These networks and associations are said to constitute 'social capital' which provides rural households with additional resources for the construction of viable livelihoods (Scoones 1998). It has also been argued that social networks play an important role in the growth of small businesses by reducing transaction costs and providing access to entrepreneurial assistance in the form of credit and expertise (Granovetter 1985; Van Dijk & Rabellotti 1997; Pedersen 1997).

Optimistic assessments of the benefits of social capital tend to gloss over the significant impact of economic differentiation and ethnic or local institutional features in determining access to relevant forms of social capital. More socially sensitive analyses have pointed out that only better-off households or households from specialized groups are actually able to deploy social networks in ways that connect them with economically relevant resources (Bryceson 2000; Gordon 1999; Meagher & Mustapha 1997). As Morton et al. note in a study of Pakistan:

> Various aspects of both "traditional" social structure and broader political economy tend to reduce the access of the rural poor to social capital. Firstly, ...the social networks of the poor link them predominantly to other poor households, and to the wealthy only through potentially exploitative patron-client relations. (cited in Gordon 1999: 6)

Among the poor, social networks only constitute a form of capital in the most metaphoric sense, since their connections often fail to provide access to the resources necessary to improve income levels or seize economic opportunities. Thus, social capital cannot simply be assumed from the existence of social interconnections and civil associations; it must be demonstrated through an analysis of the nature and level of resources to which these contacts provide access. Questions must also be raised regarding the impact of economic restructuring on the economic capacity of these forms of social capital.

The story of social capital in Nasarawan Doya tends to confirm the more pessimistic scenarios of inadequate access to resources through social networks for most poor households, despite evidence of a proliferation of local associations and inter-household networks. During the 1990s, there has been a notable increase in the number of community-based associations, which play some role in infrastructural maintenance and economic assistance to members. We will turn now to a consideration of the extent to which social networks and community associations are capable of providing support for poor rural households, and the non-farm sector in general, in the face of economic restructuring.

At the time of the study, Nasarawan Doya boasted five community-based organizations. These included the village community development organization (known as NADA), an Islamic association responsible for the maintenance and control of the village mosque, a vigilante group, a youth association and a football club. In addition, there were still vestiges of an agricultural cooperative which had collapsed with the withdrawal of state support and the escalation of fertilizer prices. With the exception of the Islamic association, all of the surviving community associations had started since the mid-1980s, and three of them were already suffering from declining membership and lack of resources owing to non-payment of dues. A fourth, the vigilante group, had been doing well, owing in part to special contributions from the village elite, but was rendered obsolete by the establishment of a police post in 1997. Only the community development association claimed to be enjoying full support, and felt it was able to fund and carry out its activities, which largely involved the maintenance through direct labour of the village road and repair of the borehole.

The rise of most of these associations since the onset of structural adjustment can only partially be attributed to a display of community spirit. State directives and funding played a significant role in the creation of both community development and youth groups, which were used by the military governments of the SAP era to extend control within the rural areas, as well as to mobilize a semblance of popular support. Youth groups in particular were actively funded under General Abacha's regime, and required to supply contingents of supporters at political rallies (Yunusa 1997). The vigilante group, as just mentioned, owed most of its support to the village elite. Thus, the impetus behind these groups, as well as the funding that sustained them, was often more state-centred than civil.

While most of these associations were oriented to the fulfilment of infrastructural or entertainment needs within the village, all had subsidiary social welfare functions, providing financial assistance to paying members in times of births, marriages, deaths or other times of need. On average, upper-stratum households were found to be over-represented in these community organizations in terms of membership and financial contributions. Average contributions of upper-stratum household heads amounted to more than three times those of their lower-stratum counterparts. As the secretary of one of the organizations noted, members who paid more received more attention from the organization in times of need. This represents yet another way in which upper-stratum households were able to lighten economic pressures and maximize control of their expenditure.

None of these community organizations appeared to provide financial assistance for productive expenditure, nor did they have the resource base to consider taking on such a task. The comparative absence of economic or occupationally based organizations was noted. No household heads were found to participate in rotating credit groups, which are not a traditional part of Hausa economic organization, and only a few traditional occupational associations existed in the village, predominantly oriented toward semi-caste-based occupations such as barbers and butchers. There was undoubtedly some participation in traders' associations by resident long-distance grain, kola or livestock traders, but these were not turned up in the sample. In fact, across the various samples, the only organizations uncovered that were oriented toward the promotion of productive, particularly non-farm, activities were the home-town associations of the Igbo migrants, which met in neighbouring rural towns.

Women did not participate in these public community organizations, and no village-level women's group existed. Aside from kinship networks, the only form of social networks in which local women participated were women's friendship networks, which represented an important source of assistance involving joint ceremonial expenditure and reciprocal gift-giving; and women's rotating credit groups, which were noted more for their collapse than for their persistence. Participation in friendship networks was slightly weighted toward upper-stratum women, as was the negligible level of participation in rotating credit groups. While only two women in the household sub-sample participated in rotating credit groups, 18, representing over 25% of the sample, reported having left rotating credit groups since the early 1990s, owing to a lack of funds for the payment of contributions or owing to the collapse of the entire group. Some women maintained that their non-farm incomes were too small to support participation in rotating credit groups. This corroborates the findings mentioned earlier regarding the trend toward the collapse of women's rotating credit groups under the pressures of structural adjustment.

In general, structural adjustment has done more to limit rather than to promote participation in and the economic effectiveness of social networks and community-based associations. In the face of rising transport costs and declining real incomes, a majority of both household heads and wives indicated that they had cut back on contact with urban relatives. Demands for assistance had become concentrated on rural relatives, who were often little better off than those seeking financial help. Over one-third of household heads and wives also indicated that high costs of transport and gifts had forced them to cut back on visits to rural relatives as well. Over 40% of wives claimed to have cut back on ceremony attendance generally, and over 70% said they had cut back on the level of gifts provided. Although women had become increasingly dependent on assistance from relatives, three-quarters of wives indicated that they had been forced to cut back on the level of assistance they provided to their relatives. Despite the economic importance of ceremony attendance, women found their incomes unable to meet up with the rising cost of ceremonial gifts, complicated by increasing competition from economic needs within the household. Many resorted to pooling money to buy a single gift, or just gave cash, which accounts for the higher level of cash received as gifts among lower-stratum women. When it is remembered that visits, assistance, ceremony attendance and gifts constitute the main forms of investment in rural social networks, these cutbacks in social expenditure take on increasing significance.

Overall, lower-stratum households appeared less able to maintain their participation in social networks, while being the most in need of their assistance. Thus, the increasing economic importance of social networks has tended to reinforce rather than to moderate economic differentiation in Nasarawan Doya. Moreover, rural social networks and community organizations have shown little capacity to compensate for declining transfers of physical resources from the state, particularly among poorer households, who are least able to meet up with dues. By contrast, the Igbo commercial networks appear to be weathering the ravages of economic restructuring owing to their much stronger institutional basis. Rather than being thrown up as an emergency response to the demands of economic restructuring, as is the case of many of the community associations of Nasarawan Doya, the Igbo commercial networks were already deeply embedded in the structure of both Igbo and Nigerian society long before the advent of structural adjustment (Forrest 1994). While not immune to the economic pressures of adjustment, they dispose of a wider range of institutional and economic resources for responding to these pressures. They also provide resources that are particularly tailored to the needs of non-farm sector growth, such as skills training, credit, and supply networks. Such resources are conspicuously lacking in most of the associations and networks available to rural indigenes of Nasarawan Doya.

8

Conclusion

The task of this study was to provide a link between very localized developments in a single village, and the wider regional, national and even global processes that frame the development of the rural non-farm sector in Africa. The aim of this approach was to grasp both the ways in which wider processes of social change and economic restructuring have shaped localized patterns of non-farm development, and the ways in which local social, economic and agro-ecological factors have shaped, or constrained, the impact of global processes and policy initiatives. At worst, this analysis has provided a basis for a more general understanding of the policy needs of the non-farm sector in a particular rural environment; at best, it has challenged some of the conventional assumptions about the contemporary role of the non-farm sector in Africa, with a view to reassessing the accompanying policy agenda. The task that remains is to address the policy implications of the study through a summary of the central findings, and an assessment of their economic and policy implications for the development of the non-farm sector in the Nigerian savanna.

Current trends in the role of the non-farm sector

Among the most basic lessons of this study is that, in the context of northern Nigeria, the pressures contributing to the expansion of the non-farm sector are linked to the need for capital, rather than to shortages of land or labour. While there is evidence of the closing of the land frontier, and some development of land shortage among junior males, land distribution at the household level was not found to be strongly associated with levels of agricultural income or with recourse to non-farm sources of income. In the case of labour, the impact of land shortage on the economic strategies of junior males, combined with the economic pressures of structural adjustment on local farmers and rural migrants, appears to have overcome the traditional labour constraint once characteristic of northern Nigerian agriculture, such that in the 1990s access to labour was not perceived to be a major problem. The critical factor underlying the apparent expansion of the non-farm sector in the Nigerian savanna relates to developments in the terms of trade in grain-based agriculture, particularly to the capital constraint created by rising production costs and cost of living inflation in the face of unstable and increasingly inadequate increases in the price of relevant cash crops.

A snapshot of current trends in individual as well as household livelihood strategies suggests an expansion in the significance of non-farm activities under these conditions. In Nasarawan Doya, non-farm activities were found to account for 60% of household incomes in cash and kind, and an average of 36% of men's and women's working hours in the course of the agricultural year, with comparatively little variation between socio-economic strata. Perhaps more significantly, non-farm activities were found to account for over one-half of men's annual incomes, and nearly a third of male incomes during the wet season, the main season of agricultural activity. While this appears, at first glance, to suggest that non-farm activities may have begun to compete with agriculture for resources and labour time, evidence on investment flows between the agricultural and non-farm sectors suggests the opposite. The unexpected observation that the season with the lowest level of agricultural activity also had the lowest level of non-farm activity highlighted the high level of dependence of non-farm activities, for their inputs, their investible capital, and their markets, on the activities and economic cycle of agriculture.

In terms of resource use, the non-farm sector remains essentially complementary with agriculture, such that households with buoyant agricultural incomes tend to be those who have benefitted most from developments in the non-farm sector, and vice-versa. Households that were agriculturally better-off were better able to seize new opportunities and overcome the inflationary pressures of adjustment both in agriculture and in the non-farm sector. By contrast, households suffering from inadequate levels of agricultural production lacked the resources to make timely shifts in or out of non-farm activities in the face of changing economic conditions, and found themselves increasingly concentrated in low capital, low return activities. Particularly among poor households and youth, non-farm activities played an important role in maintaining, and in some cases consolidating, a foothold in agriculture. Young males, in particular, used non-farm incomes to generate resources for the acquisition of land, though rising costs made land acquisition extremely difficult once males acquired the responsibility of supporting a household.

In general, many of the same constraints that account for inadequate agricultural incomes among poor households – lack of capital, inadequate control of household labour – also undermine their ability to take advantage of non-farm opportunities. It is only by overcoming the former that individuals as well as households have been able to benefit from the latter. These findings support the contention of the literature that, in the context of rural Africa, non-farm activities tend to aggravate rural inequality, since it is better-off rather than poorer households who tend to benefit from opportunities for diversification (Haggblade et al. 1989; Saith 1992; Dercon & Krishnan 1996; Reardon et al. 2000).

The one dimension of the non-farm sector that appeared to display a tendency to dampen the differentiating impact of non-farm earnings, namely women's non-farm incomes, may find its positive impact on rural income inequality undermined by a context of rising input costs and increasing competition in the narrow range of activities accessible to women. These economic pressures on women's incomes are exacerbated by an increasing tendency among male household heads from the poorer strata to shift additional burdens of household reproduction onto women. The poor are similarly disadvantaged by the impact of economic hardship on access to social networks. While encouraging increased recourse to economic assistance through social networks, the pressures of structural adjustment have also tended to undermine the capacity of poor households to maintain access to such networks.

Long-term trends in non-farm income shares

Regarding trends in the importance of non-farm incomes in household incomes, the data from Nasarawan Doya appear to confirm earlier impressions based on time-series data from the nearby village of Rogo (Table 2.1). If women's incomes are excluded from the Nasarawan Doya data in order to increase comparability with the Rogo data, non-farm income shares have risen from 36% to roughly 55% of total household incomes between 1974/5-1996/7, and from 56% to 59% of total cash incomes. This indicates a significant rise in the non-farm share of total household income in cash and kind, and a continued fluctuation of the non-farm share of household *cash* incomes within a band 50-60%. Two different forces appear to be at work here. The significant rise in the non-farm share of *total incomes* appears to derive from the increasing commercialization of rural life in the savanna area. In the process, however, non-farm sources of *cash income* do not appear to have gained significantly in importance relative to agricultural sources since the mid-1970s. They have continued to fluctuate between 50-60%, rising and falling in response to the framework of economic and policy incentives. The data on non-farm shares of cash incomes in Rogo and Nasarawan Doya are summarized in Figure 8.1.

However, behind the trend toward rising non-farm shares of total income, and relatively stable shares of cash income, a different story can be told from a consideration of the disaggregated data. Disaggregated by socio-economic stratum, the data suggest that critical changes have taken place

Figure 8.1 Changes in Non-Farm Income

Shares in the Nigerian Savanna, 1974-1996

(% of Household Cash Income)

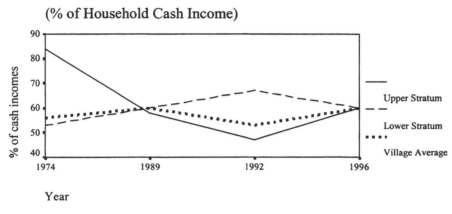

Year

All data exclude women's incomes.

All data include agricultural wage labour as 'non-farm' income.

Data for 1974-92 refer to the village of Rogo, while data for 1996 are taken from the nearby village of Nasarawan Doya.

since 1992. Rather than simply fluctuating in response to agricultural policy trends, the 1996 data on non-farm shares of cash incomes for upper and lower stratum households show a dramatic change from their previous trajectories. While upper stratum households showed a consistent decline in the non-farm share of cash incomes from 1974-1992, the data for 1996 shows a noticeable increase. Conversely, lower stratum households, who showed a consistent rise in dependence on non-farm incomes as a source of cash between 1974 and 1992, have shifted toward a marked decline in 1996. These reversals suggest that there has been a decisive change in 1996 relative to previous years. It could be argued that the change is due to the fact that the earlier data are all from the village of Rogo, and the final set are from Nasarawan Doya. However, the proximity of the two villages, their similarities in terms of population and levels of commercialization, and the pervasive agro-ecological and socio-economic similarities that exist between them, would tend to militate against such an explanation.

The most probable explanation lies, rather, in the marked decline in terms of trade in commercial grain production since 1992, combined with the impact of economic restructuring on access to non-farm incomes. Following some 15 years of generally favourable conditions in commercial grain production, upper stratum households have responded to the recent decline in agricultural terms of trade, as well as the emergence of some profitable non-farm opportunities, by shifting their income-generating strategies in favour of the non-farm sector. In other words, upper stratum households have responded to push factors in agriculture by turning attention to pull factors within the non-farm sector. By contrast, lower-stratum households, who turned increasingly to non-farm incomes from the mid-1970s to compensate for their more precarious access to agricultural livelihoods, are now faced with declining access to non-farm incomes as well. In the context of intensified pressures on agricultural livelihoods since the early 1990s, rising costs of non-farm participation, and increased competition within the non-farm sector, lower-stratum households are caught between push factors in agriculture and push factors in the non-farm sector. In short, the livelihood strategies of lower stratum households are being pushed to the wall.

The incorporation of women's incomes into this data would tend to accentuate rather than moderate the picture. Although in 1996 non-farm incomes of lower-stratum women were still found to contribute more to household income, both proportionately and absolutely, than incomes of upper-stratum women, women's incomes were found to be under increasing pressure owing to lack of capital, increasing economic pressures within the household, increasing competition, and weak markets. Moreover, lower-stratum women were more severely affected by these pressures than upper-stratum women. Nor does the development of new income-generating opportunities under structural adjustment seem set to change these patterns.

New opportunities in the non-farm sector have tended on the whole to be men's opportunities, and the few lucrative possibilities available to women were found to require levels of capital that made them inaccessible to lower-stratum households. This suggests that the moderating effect of women's non-farm incomes on rural income inequality is likely to decrease, accentuating the trends toward rural differentiation and stagnating non-farm incomes among lower-stratum households.

Although this constitutes a very localized and tentative analysis of long-term trends in non-farm participation, it raises issues that should be taken seriously in light of increasingly optimistic claims regarding the economic potential of the non-farm sector. The fact that this interpretation of the data is backed by considerable historical evidence underlines its claim to serious consideration. If nothing else, it helps to illuminate a critical lacuna in the literature on 'push' and 'pull' factors, by addressing the question of what happens to households who are affected by push factors, but lack the resources to respond to pull factors. Reardon et al. (1998) give the impression that such households are simply unable to enter the non-farm sector. The evidence presented here suggests otherwise. Driven by pressures on agricultural livelihoods, poor households have no choice but to enter the non-farm sector on increasingly disadvantageous terms, which show up as declining access to non-farm incomes despite high levels of non-farm participation.

To address the issue of 'de-agrarianization', the long-term evidence presented here suggests that there is no overall trend away from agricultural livelihoods in the Nigerian savanna. What appears to be taking place is a movement in and out of agricultural livelihoods in response to shifts in agricultural policy and terms of trade. This pattern is perhaps easier to discern in the northern Nigerian context, where both positive and negative shifts in agricultural terms of trade have occurred since the 1970s. In many other African countries, trends in agricultural terms of trade have been more consistently negative over the same period, which would tend to reinforce a perception of a secular decline in dependence on agriculture. However, in the northern Nigerian context, this flexible response to economic and policy conditions is taking place largely within the upper stratum of farming households, who have the resources to make timely and profitable changes.

By contrast, the lower stratum of rural households have found the terms of trade generated by agricultural and economic policy consistently unfavourable to local resource-poor agricultural production since the early colonial period, and have been increasingly forced to turn to a range of non-farm income sources by default. In their case, however, any tendency toward de-agrarianization is limited by the lack of viable economic options. The apparent shift away from agricultural sources of livelihood is taking place without any expanding process of industrialization or capitalist farming to absorb their labour, and without the resources or skills to create adequately viable small-scale alternatives of their own. The fragile livelihoods that result appear increasingly unsustainable in the context of economic restructuring, reinforcing, rather than undermining, the commitment of poorer households to the 'subsistence fall-back' of agricultural production (Bryceson 1999). Not only can this process not be characterized as de-agrarianization; it cannot, without significant external input, constitute a dynamic force for rural development.

Future prospects for the non-farm sector: Theoretical issues and research concerns

This brings us to the broader question: Whither the non-farm sector? Are we faced with a process capable of taking the economic lead in rural development, or with a degenerative process based on economic desperation and unproductive survival strategies? What are the implications of developments in the non-farm sector for the future of rural diversification? For the development of agriculture? For rural accumulation and household welfare? Answers to some of these questions will be explored through an assessment of future prospects for non-farm development in relation to five major issues: agriculture, rural inequality, new non-farm opportunities, small rural towns, and social networks.

To begin with the issue of agriculture, this study adds its voice to the growth linkages literature in emphasizing the primacy of agriculture in the development of a dynamic non-farm sector. The study has shown that the adequacy of agricultural production to household consumption and cash needs determines the economic terms on which household members participate in the non-farm sector. The timing of non-farm participation, its impact on household agricultural performance, the capital for entering low-return or high-return activities – in short, whether non-farm activities are pursued as low-income survival strategies or as income maximization strategies with a potential for accumulation and re-investment in agriculture – all are heavily influenced by the agricultural base of rural households. At the sectoral level, agriculture plays a central role in the generation of non-farm opportunities, the formation of non-farm capital, and the creation of effective demand for non-farm goods and services. To suppose that the non-farm sector can provide an independent impetus for development in the context of a crisis-ridden agricultural sector, a withdrawn state, and declining access to urban incomes, is to believe in the possibility of creating something from nothing.

In the absence of greater attention to the development of household agriculture, the expansion of the non-farm sector looks set to intensify, rather than alleviate, rural poverty and income inequality. In the face of increasingly negative agricultural terms of trade and declining agricultural incomes, not to mention rising costs of entry into the non-farm sector, the rural poor will find themselves increasingly concentrated in labour intensive, low-income non-farm activities, in which incomes are largely unsuccessful in keeping up with the rising cost of living, of agricultural production and of non-farm participation. Reardon et al. (2000) have recognized this risk by noting that current macro-economic conditions are likely to intensify barriers to entry into non-farm activities. The evidence presented above on long-term trends in the share of non-farm incomes suggests that even the limited welfare function that non-farm incomes have played in the past is under threat in the face of growing competition from better-endowed rural households and urban outsiders. The more successful non-farm endeavours of these better-endowed actors should not be allowed to eclipse the much larger proportion of barely viable non-farm activities, nor should it be allowed to obscure the destabilizing effects of a pattern of non-farm development that intensifies rural income inequality.

The image of non-farm dynamism created by the emergence of new economic opportunities under structural adjustment also requires closer analysis. While new opportunities have undoubtedly been created, an assessment of their economic prospects requires a consideration of the nature of those opportunities and their long term economic prospects. Two types of new opportunities can be distinguished, those related to the provision of infrastructural and welfare services formerly provided by the state, and those derived from changes in the supply and demand for privately provided goods and services.

At the level of rural services, it is important to distinguish between the failure or elimination of public provision, and the creation of private economic opportunities. The former relates only to a cessation of supply, while the latter requires that the gap in supply be accompanied by the existence of effective demand. The problematic experience of cost-recovery programmes in Africa, and their frequently negative impact of the use of public services, suggests that the economic opportunities created by the collapse of rural public services are likely to be limited. Add to this the context of declining real incomes, particularly in food-crop agriculture, and the prospects for private service provision appear even slimmer. In Nasarawan Doya, gaps in public service provision were more commonly met by the formation of community associations than by the emergence of private service providers. Moreover, low cost communal provision was both poor in quality and difficult for many households to afford. Where services could not be communally organized, such as in the areas of health and water provision when the borehole broke down, private provision generally involved reversion to low-cost, labour intensive traditional options, such as water carriers and traditional medicine. Both the skills and the capital for local provision of modern services were largely absent. Even where better-endowed outsiders moved in to offer modern services through the private sector, such as in the area of health care, the level of effective demand proved too low to sustain them.

The other category of new opportunities relates to how the contraction of the urban economy affects the demand for rural goods and services, which may act as a substitute for imported and urban industrial goods and services.

In the case of Nasarawan Doya, the developmental potential of this type of new opportunity is also severely limited. The profitability of these economic opportunities is based on increased demand for inferior goods and local retailing in the face of a contraction of real incomes, rather than on any genuine competitive edge derived from cheaper labour or specialized skills. Low levels of education, skills, infrastructure and effective demand leave very little scope for the emergence of more competitive or highly skilled activities such as Fisher et al. (1997) have noted in rural India. Moreover, given the foundation of these opportunities in weakened effective demand, the level of profitability of these activities does not appear able to support any significant new investment or technical development. Local sugar production was dependent on second-hand obsolete machinery, and was unable to support the cost of local production of that machinery. The bakery represented an attempt to exploit abandoned facilities, not to undertake new investment. Even the local blacksmith was unable to parlay increased demand for locally produced tools and local mechanical repairs into new investment in the production of bicycle carriers for a wider market.

These observations suggest, on the one hand, that policy makers need to make a distinction between 'opportunistic' new opportunities, which simply exploit changes in demand based on economic hardship, and 'developmental' new opportunities, which compete on the basis of something other than inferior quality or reduced quantity, and have some scope for technical development or innovation. On the other hand, it suggests that the latter type of new opportunity demands a minimum level of skills, infrastructure and investment that are sorely lacking in the rural environment of the northern Nigerian savanna, and in many other areas of Africa.

A sound analysis of the prospects of the non-farm sector requires more effective differentiation among types of non-farm activities, not just by subsector, but in terms of their economic potential. Fisher et al. (1997) have taken a useful step in this direction with their three-way categorization of non-farm activities in terms of their share of employment and growth potential. More research is needed into the factors that influence growth potential of particular non-farm activities in various regions, with a view to targetting interventions at activities with economic potential rather than simply focussing on reducing barriers to entry regardless of the absorptive capacity or growth potential of a given activity.

There is also need for a hard look at the rather trendy issues of reverse migration and the role of small rural towns in non-farm enterprise growth. The prevailing hypothesis envisions a reverse migration of skilled labour toward the rural areas and the clustering of rural enterprise at the level of small rural towns (Æroe 1992; Baker & Pedersen 1992; Pedersen 1997). From the perspective of Nasarawan Doya, the reality appears to be precisely the opposite. Far from returning skills and capital to the rural areas, reverse migration brings home only the poorest and the least skilled labour. Better-endowed migrants continue to hang on in the urban informal sector if they are unable to gain, or retain, a foothold in the formal sector. Not only does the urban informal sector tend to retain local out-migrants with any viable level of skills or capital, it is also full to bursting with better skilled migrants from other regions, who can consider relocation into the rural hinterland without the stigma of failure. The upshot is that the urban informal sector, largely ignored in much of the rural small-town literature, becomes a key source of competition for new economic opportunities in the rural areas. Moreover, the entrepreneurs most likely to respond to rural non-farm opportunities are not locals from the hinterland, but non-locals.

Available evidence suggests that small rural towns, only recently dis-covered by development theorists, were discovered very early in the struc-tural adjustment period by entrepreneurs from the urban informal sector, who began shifting their enterprises down to smaller towns as urban markets became increasingly saturated (Meagher & Yunusa 1996). In Nasarawan Doya, the rural non-farm sector in northern villages has become the final commercial frontier for young southern Nigerian entrepreneurs from the towns, who find themselves unable to compete in saturated urban and small-town markets. Thus, in the context of structural adjustment, the prevailing direction of enterprise movements has been from the urban areas down to the smaller towns and villages, rather than the reverse. Far from acting as an incubator for rural non-farm enterprise, small rural towns appear to function more as stepping-stones for urban informal entrepreneurs and other out-siders to move in on economic opportunities in the rural areas.

This perspective increases the sense of the vulnerability of the rural non-farm sector to external competition. In addition to inadequate skills, weak rural markets, and a weakened agricultural resource base, the non-farm sector must contend with competition from the better skilled and resourced outsiders from the urban informal sector, who are already scanning the rural horizon for signs of economic opportunity. While infrastructural improvements may increase the level of outside competition in the rural non-farm sector, the economic pressures of structural adjustment have already breached the protective wall of rural economic isolation.

This evidence suggests that more needs to be known about the process of clustering in small rural towns. Where are clustering entrepreneurs coming from, and what attracts them to rural towns? Has economic restructuring triggered a trend toward increased penetration of ethnic outsiders into the rural areas? Does infrastructural development in small rural towns, or between small towns and villages, facilitate or impede such a process (by enabling local rural enterprises to face external competition). The current focus on trust and collective efficiency yields very little useful information on the migratory dynamics underlying the formation of small-town clusters (van Dijk & Rabellotti 1997; McCormick & Pedersen 1996). There is a need for greater empirical investigation of these issues, rather than relying on dualistic models of rural-urban economic relations to deduce rather than investigate the impact of macro-economic change (Meagher 1999).

A greater awareness of the hidden institutional logics underlying non-farm development can be seen in the greater sensitivity to the role of social networks. Unfortunately, much of the literature on this institutional dimension of non-farm development has tended to go too far in the opposite direction. There has been a strong propensity, particularly among proponents of sustainable rural livelihoods, to treat social networks or 'social capital' as a kind of universal resource possessed by all individuals, households and communities – a resource which can make up for shortfalls in financial or human capital, or substitute for withdrawn public services. This position has been effectively criticised by Deborah Bryceson (2000). As this study and many others have demonstrated, it is the institutional content of these networks and associations, rather than the mere fact of their existence, that determines whether they can contribute to enterprise development or public service provision. While most rural dwellers participate in some form of social network, the question is whether the type of assistance accessible through such networks is adequate, or even relevant, to the seeker's livelihood or entrepreneurial needs. Access to *effective* social networks, far from being a universally available resource, is extremely uneven across regional, socio-economic and gender categories (Edwards & Foley 1997). Questions need to be raised about the types of social networks that are useful for non-farm development, and about the determinants of access to such networks, and about the impact of economic restructuring on the institutional capacity of these networks.

The case of Nasarawan Doya has shown that community associations with shallow roots, and the personal networks of the poor, do little to assist in the provision of local services and even less in the development of viable non-farm enterprises. This is particularly so under conditions of economic stress. By contrast, commercial networks and other informal economic institutions that are well-rooted in the local social structure can provide significant technical and economic support to members, as in the case of the Igbo networks. Before deciding whether these informal institutional resources can be replicated, it is important to understand a little more about what allows them to develop and how they operate. It is also important to investigate where commercially oriented networks have in fact developed – in which areas, ethnic groups or activities do they operate, and in which are they absent? This can provide important indicators as to where, and in which activities, existing social infrastructure for enterprise development can be drawn upon. It is equally important to recognize where such informal economic infrastructure does not exist or exists only weakly, and to take this as a guide to the types of formal intervention that may be required for entrepreneurial development. A great deal more research is needed into the informal insitutional context that underpins the growth of the non-farm sector, with a view to replacing the blind confidence that appears to have been placed in its capacities, with a more realistic assessment of its potential in different contexts.

Policy reflections

The findings of this study suggest that the non-farm sector cannot, as Saith (1992) has argued, function as a panacea for failed industrialization drives and declining agricultural incomes. Even in the agriculturally and entrepreneurially active context of the Nigerian savanna, concerted policy attention to agriculture as well as to rural small-scale enterprise development will be required to transform the non-farm sector from a developmental placebo into a dynamic force in the rural development process. Rather than attempting to work out a package of concrete recommendations, this final section will focus on raising key policy issues, and, where relevant, contextualizing them with regard to current developments in the Nigerian savanna.

The first policy recommendation of most of the orthodox non-farm literature is to re-emphasize the need for an 'enabling environment' (Gordon 1999; Lanjouw 1999; Reardon et al. 1998). This refers to the standard macro-economic package of structural adjustment policies: devaluation, deregulation, removal of subsidies and state withdrawal from social service provision. These recommendations are normally backed up with stylized anecdotal evidence of how such policies ought to promote the non-farm sector, but rarely is any evidence provided as to whether they have actually promoted any form of broad-based non-farm income growth, despite some twenty years' experience with structural adjustment throughout rural Africa. Moreover, no account is taken of the effects of adjustment policies on agriculture, despite constant reaffirmation that a healthy agriculture is essential to a dynamic non-farm sector. While the macro-economic environment is indeed critical to the success of non-farm development, evidence from Nasarawan Doya suggests that structural adjustment policies have created what can only be described as a 'disabling environment' for both agriculture and for the non-farm sector. Far from providing macro-economic stability, adjustment policies have brought with them massive price instability and economic uncertainty, which have only intensified as the idiosyncratic bans and subsidies of the original Nigerian version of structural adjustment have been removed. The negative effect of structural adjustment on food crop agriculture has undermined access to capital for non-farm investment as well as enfeebling the key market for non-farm goods and services. In addition, devaluation and price liberalization have weakened access to inputs and equipment for non-farm activities, as well as intensifying competition within the low-income sub-sectors.

In the context of low-resource, technically under-developed household agriculture – particularly in the case of food crop agriculture – policy recommendations for non-farm development must depart from the liberalizing requirements of the mainstream literature. If the idea is to develop a dynamic non-farm sector capable of improving rural incomes without a destabilizing acceleration of rural inequality, this must be premised on measures to promote small-scale agriculture, on which the viability of most non-farm options is dependent. Sustainable rural livelihood approaches which focus on limiting vulnerability and insulating rural livelihoods against external shocks tend to ignore the importance of agriculture to the viability of economic alternatives. Even worse, they ignore the integration of rural households into wider systems of regional and national production. In critical food production areas such as the Nigerian savanna, attempts at the insulation of rural livelihoods are not only meaningless, but may generate new shocks as local livelihood strategies feed into the national food and agro-input system. Policies to promote viable rural livelihoods must therefore focus on increasing the productivity and profitability of peasant agriculture in the food crop sector, not at withdrawal into a range of agricultural and non-agricultural survival strategies.

In the context of the Nigerian savanna, key policy measures to promote agriculture would include the reimposition of controls on grain imports, the maintenance of some measure of subsidy on fertilizer and pesticides, and concerted improvements in the distribution of fertilizer, both subsidized and unsubsidized. Greater liberalization may be needed in the organization of fertilizer distribution, although this would have to be carefully coordinated if any measure of subsidy is to be maintained. In the period since the completion of the fieldwork for this study, these policy concerns have been overtaken by events, and then some. In 1997, shortly before the conclusion of the fieldwork, the distribution of fertilizer was fully liberalized and the subsidy completely removed – measures which greatly increased the availability of fertilizer (though not always of the required type and quality), but failed to reduce the cost sufficiently to significantly improve access on the part of small farmers. This represented one of the last in a series of liberalizing measures which, between 1992 and 1998, removed all of the key illiberal components of Nigeria's original Structural Adjustment Programme, including the import bans on grain, and the subsidies on fertilizer and petrol. However, this 'proper' liberalization programme has been followed, since the death of General Abacha in mid-1997, by a total reversal in the agricultural policy direction. In January 1999, bans were re-imposed on the importation of wheat flour, maize, sorghum and millet with a view to boosting local agricultural production (IRIN no. 2, 1.5.99). In the course of the 1999 planting season, a moderate 25% subsidy was reimposed on a limited quantity of fertilizer, and the question of fertilizer pricing and distribution has been reopened.

It is, as yet, too early to assess the impact of these measures on local agriculture, or on non-farm development, but they offer at least some potential for easing the crippling trends in agricultural terms of trade which have tended to undermine the viability of both agriculture and the non-farm sector in northern Nigeria. This change in policy direction represents a recognition on the part of the democratically elected Obasanjo regime that, although the fiscal implications of a more interventionist agricultural strategy are considerable, they are not, in the long run, as considerable as the costs of allowing the bulk of rural farming households to be further marginalized by agricultural policy. Although thirty years of inappropriate state intervention have failed to develop small-scale agriculture in Nigeria (Watts 1987), it cannot then be concluded that exposure to global competitive forces will do the job. Indeed, a little critical thinking makes it clear that precisely because previous interventionist policies have failed, Nigeria's small-scale agriculturalists are completely unable to face global competition. What is needed to create a healthy agricultural base is not liberalization, but *appropriate* intervention that focuses on bringing agricultural productivity up to the level that will enable it to face a more liberalized environment.

Although policy measures to improve agricultural terms of trade are a necessary condition for productive expansion of the non-farm sector, they are by no means sufficient conditions. Specific policy measures are also needed to address problems of access and effective resource use within the non-farm sector itself. While increased agricultural incomes may help to generate capital for limited non-farm investment and buoy up rural effective demand, the underdevelopment of skills and rural infrastructure, and the lack of access to appropriate technology, technical services and adequate levels of finance will continue to constitute a serious impediment to the development of the non-farm sector. A dizzying succession of organizations for the development and provision of improved rural technologies, as well as the provision of loans, training and back-up services have existed in Nigeria, along with various agencies for the development and rehabilitation of rural infrastructure. The current repertoire includes the newly formed Department of Rural Development (DRD), which is centrally concerned with the promotion of the rural non-farm sector; the recently scrapped (but still sporadically operating) Family Economic Advancement Programme (FEAP), which has dealt in loans and equipment; the Agricultural and Rural Management Training Institute (ARMTI) and Agricultural Mechanization Programme of the Institute of Agricultural Research, which focus on the development of appropriate non-farm technologies; and numerous NGO programmes for rural income generation and the economic empowerment of women.

The virtual absence of the services of these organizations, or any of their predecessors, in Nasarawan Doya is a clear indicator of their relevance to the vast majority of Nigerian rural entrepreneurs. However, the replication of these non-farm development initiatives is not likely to improve matters. What is needed are improved coordination of the activities of these various organizations, as well as efforts to improve the effectiveness of existing programmes for the needs of non-farm development. Nigeria has already recognized the need for coordination of non-farm development initiatives across a range of departments, ministries and non-state organizations. The DRD has attempted to identify existing government and non-government agencies involved in any aspect of non-farm development, across Ministerial and state boundaries, with a view to coordinating rather than duplicating their activities. Efforts are also being made to promote private sector involvement in relevant aspects of non-farm development, though the scope for effective private sector involvement is currently fairly narrow, given the low level of rural purchasing power.

As for measures to improve the effectiveness of non-farm development initiatives, the DRD seems keen to learn from past mistakes. In Nigeria, the mistakes made in non-farm development initiatives mirror fairly closely the problems cited in wider literature. First is the lack of attention to the development of appropriate skills (Bryceson 2000; Reardon et al 1998; Gordon 1999). A greater concern with the development of local technical and maintenance skills, and back-up services, rather than with the perfunctory provision of credit and equipment for rural income generation projects, would go a long way to improving the effectiveness of development programmes. In northern Nigeria in particular, greater emphasis on the provision of accessible primary education in the rural areas, and on addressing negative local attitudes to Western education, is also critical to the development of appropriate skills for improved access to non-farm incomes.

Secondly, there is a pressing need for greater attention to issues of demand, rather than confining policy to the conventional focus on supply-side issues. As Fisher et al. (1997: 84) point out in the case of India, policies that focus on improving access to non-farm activities without considering whether there is sufficiently elastic demand for the output of those activities, can only lead to failure:

> Promotional resources and activities are wasted if they fly in the face of the underlying demand trends, and this has led to a series of major policy failures within the context of the RNFS [rural non-farm sector]. A notorious example is the way in which policymakers have regarded the lack of credit rather than of demand as the ruling constraint, and devoted vast resources to financing unproductive activities.

Because demand conditions, and their intersection with local skill and resource endowments, vary from one area to another, the concern with the profit potential of a given activity requires greater attention to local variations in the emergence of, or potential for, new economic opportunities. The targeting of capital and equipment loans, as well as targeting the development of local technologies, on the basis of an assessment of the activities with the greatest local economic potential would help to maximize the effectiveness of such investments. The administrative and resource demands of greater sensitivity to local conditions and local technical needs are substantial, but often make the difference between money squandered and money well spent.

A third area of concern in improving the effectiveness of non-farm development programmes relates to the issue of targeting particular groups, usually women and poor households, for special policy attention. It has been noted that better-off households, and male heads, tend to have the most advantageous access to non-farm as well as agricultural incomes. Without targeting, policies to promote access to non-farm activities are likely to benefit these better-off groups disproportionately. Measures such as public works, 'poor-friendly' micro-credit and promotion of specifically female activities have been suggested (Bryceson & Howe 1995; Gordon 1999; Lanjouw 1999). However, two caveats should be raised. The first is that the kind of interventions that facilitate non-farm access for the poor are likely to be inadequate to the promotion of the new economic opportunities that have emerged in the non-farm sector in the context of economic restructuring. As the case of Nasarawan Doya has shown, these new opportunities tend to be relatively skill and capital intensive. The promotion of these 'cutting edge' non-farm opportunities is likely to require higher levels of credit and more technically advanced and specific training. The second caveat is that it should be kept in mind that recourse to non-farm activities, particularly in the case of poor households, is associated with the individuation of liveli-hood strategies among household members, arising from, and further rein-forcing, the breakdown of the economic coherence of households. Targeting of particular household members should be undertaken in conjunction with efforts to reinforce key structures of economic cooperation within the house-hold. Otherwise, these interventions run the risk of contributing to the break-down of household agriculture, which would in turn undermine a key source of non-farm capital for all household members.

This brings us to the fourth issue of non-farm development policy, which involves attention to the informal institutional framework of non-farm development in particular areas. Policy initiatives must incorporate an awareness of the types of informal institutional infrastructure that exist, or do not exist, in a particular area. Something as simple as rotating credit groups do not constitute a universal institution throughout rural Africa. They can be drawn on as a well-rooted institutional resource for credit delivery in some areas, and are weak and ineffective in others. Similarly, trading networks, apprenticeship systems and other informal economic and training institutions, may or may not exist, or may be more strongly or weakly developed in various areas, or may exist only for certain activities and not for others. The ability to identify and tap this informal economic infrastructure, and to take it into account as a potential obstacle in certain circumstances, would enormously increase the effectiveness of non-farm development interventions. The idea that policy should aim to create these 'social networks' in areas where they are found not to exist should be considered with due caution. The creation of effective informal institutions is not as low-cost an option as policy makers appear to believe. The development of new institutions, whether formal or informal, requires considerable external support, particularly where the practices are not culturally familiar. Conversely, weakly rooted institutional transplants are likely to be more wasteful of resources, and considerably less effective, than overt formal sector programmes.

A final policy issue to be considered is that of infrastructural development. This includes the improvement of road networks, rural electrification, improved access to water, and provision of appropriate market and workshop facilities. While widely recognized to play a vital role in non-farm development, there is growing concern that improvements in infrastructure may have negative side-effects. Reardon et al. (1998) have pointed out that infrastructural development is a 'double-edged sword', improving access to productive facilities and markets, but at the same time exposing the rural non-farm sector to increased external competition. Gordon (1999) has suggested that appropriate sequencing of infrastructural change may help to mitigate the negative effects. She proposes localized infrastructural provision linking small towns and villages, to be followed by linkages with urban areas once rural enclaves have reached a critical level of competitiveness. Once again, evidence from Nasarawan Doya suggests that sequencing of infrastructural change is not likely to solve the problem. The whiff of economic opportunity is enough to attract the first wave of outside competition, which is likely to be intensified as local infrastructual improvements increase the income-generating capacity of particular activities. Without concerted policy attention to the development of local technical and entrepreneurial skills, as well as access to adequate finance, improvements in infrastructure are only likely to accelerate the invasion of the non-farm sector by more competitive entrepreneurs or products from outside the rural areas.

Even the extensive measures discussed here will have only a very limited effect on the rural economy in the absence of more sustained improvements in the wider national economy. Ashwani Saith's (1992) observation, quoted at the beginning of this study, should serve as a reminder that the rural economy is an organic part of the national economy, not an isolated enclave that can disengage from national economic instability through the development of sustainable livelihoods. Just as the non-farm sector cannot grow independently of conditions in agriculture, the rural economy cannot be revived without addressing the crisis in the urban economy. Access to capital, skills and services, as well as conditions of competition within the non-farm sector, are intimately bound up with access to resources in the urban economy, and with the economic capacity of the state. Far from bypassing the weaknesses of the wider industrial economy and the state, the non-farm sector will only be further enfeebled by their economic incapacity.

These reflections call for a re-evaluation of prevailing policy prescriptions for the development of the non-farm sector, which concentrate on market liberalization and the improvement of rural infrastructure. There is a tendency to ignore the fact that the effectiveness of liberalization depends on the prior development of the financial, technical, and demand conditions for non-farm growth, which cannot be generated by the mere fact of diversification, particularly under conditions of crisis in the agricultural and national economies, nor can they be wished into being by the need to replace state involvement in rural development. Following decades of neglect, it is a flight of fancy to expect the rural economy suddenly to be able to cast aside the need for state assistance and kick-start its own development process. It is only when the non-farm sector is given the benefit of serious policy attention and adequate investment, rather than being deployed as a bargain solution to rural development problems, that a story that began as an admission of failure can end with a measure of success.

Epilogue

1998 was a good year for rain in Nasarawan Doya, and mercifully, there was fertilizer. At the height of the farming season, the village appears deserted during the day. By four o'clock, the hoard of young men on motorcycles begins to gather at the village transit point to wait for passengers. The row of young girls selling snacks huddle against the front of the lock-up stalls, waiting for their market to come in from the farms.

The bakery closed a few months ago after the local landlord tried to double the rent. The branch chemist at the entrance to the village has also closed, and the young Igbo entrepreneur has returned to work in his brother's business near the local town. The private clinic never re-opened, and the nurse who owned it has now moved all of her equipment back to Zaria. Even the female community health worker, the only one in the village, was recently retrenched. She now operates private health services from her rented room in the village, but will leave the village for good in December to marry. She feels there is not a strong enough market in the village to make it worthwhile for non-indigenes to stay on. Her departure will leave Nasarawan Doya, a village of over 12,600 people, with no trained female health worker – a serious problem in a context in which Islamic norms prevent women from being attended to by males. There are local midwives to fall back on, but they are unable to handle complications, not to mention the many serious illnesses endemic to the area. The need for local health services is acute, but it takes more than need to attract the private sector.

At least sugar production is still doing well, but now there is talk of a factory for local sugar production in Jigawa State ....

Appendix

Table A1.

Correlation of Number of Non-Farm Activities in Household with Age of Head and Labour Ratio

TOTAL NO. OF NON-FARM ACTIVITIES IN HOUSEHOLD		
	Pearson Correlation	Significance
Age of Head	111	0.272
Labour Ratio	278**	0.005

** Correlation signficant at the 0.01 level (2-tailed).

References

ÆROE, A. (1992) 'The Role of Small Towns in Regional Development in South-East Africa', in J. Baker and P. Ove Pedersen, eds., *The Rural-Urban Interface in Africa. Expansion and Adaptation*. Uppsala: Nordiska Afrikainstitutet.

ANDRÆ, G. AND BECKMAN, B. (1987) *Industry Goes Farming: The Nigerian Raw Material Crisis and the Case of Textiles and Cotton*. Uppsala: Scandanavian Institute of African Studies.

BAGACHWA, M.D. AND STEWART, FRANCIS (1992) 'Rural Industries and Rural Linkages in Sub-Saharan Africa: A Survey', in F. Stewart, S. Lall and S. Wangwe, eds., *Alternative Development Strategies in SubSaharan Africa*. London: Macmillan.

BAIER, S. (1980) *An Economic History of Central Niger*. Oxford: Clarendon Press.

BAKER, J. AND PEDERSEN, P.O. (1992) 'Introduction', in J. Baker and P. Ove Pedersen, eds., *The Rural-Urban Interface in Africa*. Expansion and Adaptation. Uppsala: Nordiska Afrikainstitutet.

BAKER, J. AND PEDERSEN, P.O., eds. (1992) *The Rural-Urban Interface in Africa*. Uppsala Nordiska Africainstitutet.

BECKMAN, B. (1987) 'Public Investment and Agrarian Transformation in Northern Nigeria' in M. Watts, ed., *State, Oil and Agriculture in Nigeria*. Berkeley, California: Institute of International Studies.

BELLO, S. (1982) "State and Economy in Kano 1894-1960: A Study of Colonial Domination", Ph.D. Thesis, ABU, Zaria.

BERKVENS, RONALD J.A. (1997) 'Backing Two Horses: Interaction of Agricultural and Non-Agricultural Household Activities in a Zimbabwean Communal Area'. Leiden: Afrika-Studiecentrum, Working Paper vol. 24.

BERRY, S. (1989) 'Social Institutions and Access to Resources', *Africa* 59 (1), 41-53.

BERRY, S. (1993a) *No Condition is Permanent: The Social Dynamics of Agrarian Change in Sub-Saharan Africa*. Madison: University of Wisconsin Press.

BERRY, S. (1993b) 'Coping with Confusion: African Farmers' Responses to Economic Instability in the 1970s and 1980s', in T.M. Callaghy and J. Ravenhill, eds., *Hemmed In: Responses to Africa's Economic Decline*. New York: Columbia University Press.

173

174

BRATTON, M. (1989) 'Beyond the State: Civil Society and Associational Life in Africa', *World Politics* XLI(3).

BRAUTIGAM, D. (1997) 'Substituting for the State: Institutions and Industrial Development in Eastern Nigeria', *World Development* 25(7), 1063-1080.

BRYCESON, DEBORAH F. (1996) 'Deagrarianization and Rural Employment in sub-Saharan Africa: A Sectoral Perspective', *World Development* 24 (1), 97-111.

BRYCESON, DEBORAH F. (1997) 'De-agrarianisation: Blessing or Blight?', in D.F. Bryceson and V. Jamal, eds., *Farewell to Farms: De-Agrarianisation and Employment in Africa.* Aldershot: Ashgate.

BRYCESON, DEBORAH F. (1999) 'Sub-Saharan Africa Betwixt and Between: Rural Livelihood Practices and Policies', paper presented at workshop on 'Between Town and Country: Livelihoods, Settlement and Identity Formation in Sub-Saharan Africa', June 27-30, Rhodes University, East London Campus.

BRYCESON, DEBORAH F. (2000) 'Disappearing Peasantries? Rural Labour Redundancy in the Neo-liberal Era and Beyond', in Deborah Bryceson, Cristobal Kay and Jos Mooji, eds. *Disappearing Peasantries? Rural Labour in Africa, Asia and Latin America.* London: Intermediate Technology Publications.

BRYCESON, DEBORAH F. AND HOWE, JOHN (1995) 'An Agrarian Continent in Transition', in S. Ellis, ed., *Africa Now: People, Policies and Institutions.* London: James Currey.

BRYCESON, DEBORAH F. AND JAMAL, VALI, eds. (1997) *Farewell to Farms: De-Agrarianisation and Employment in Africa.* Aldershot: Ashgate.

BYERLEE, D., EICHER, C.K., LIEDHOLM, C. AND SPENSER, D.S.C. (1977) 'Rural Employment in Tropical Africa: Summary of Findings', African Rural Economy Program, Working Paper No. 20, Michigan State University, Michigan and Njala University College, Sierra Leone.

CENTRAL BANK OF NIGERIA. *Annual Report and Statement of Accounts* (1988-1996), Lagos.

CLOUGH, P. AND WILLIAMS, G. (1987) 'Decoding Berg: The World Bank in Rural Northern Nigeria', in M. Watts, ed., *State, Oil and Agriculture in Nigeria.* Berkeley, California: Institute of International Studies.

COHEN, A. (1969) *Custom and Politics in Urban Africa. A Study of Hausa Migrants in Yoruba Towns.* London: Routledge and Kegan Paul.

DAVIES, S. (1996) *Adaptable Livelihoods. Coping with Food Insecurity in the Malian Sahel.* London: Macmillan.

DELGADO, C., HAZELL, P., HOPKINS, J., AND KELLY, V. (1994) 'Promoting Intersectoral Growth Linkages in Rural Africa Through Agricultural Technology Policy Reform', *American Journal of Agricultural Economics* 76, 1166-1171.

DERCON, S. AND KRISHNAN, P. (1996) 'Income Portfolios in Rural Ethiopia and Tanzania: Choices and Constraints' *Journal of Development Studies* 32 (6), 850-875.

DIKE, E. (1994) 'Economic Development, Urban Labour Absorption and the Informal Sector in Nigeria', mimeo, Ahmadu Bello University, Zaria, Nigeria.

EDWARDS, BOB AND FOLEY, M. (1997) 'Social Capital and the Political Economy of Our Discontent', in B. Edwards and M. Foley, eds., *Social Capital, Civil Society, and Contemporary Democracy*, American Behavioral Scientist 40 (5) 669-678.

EGG, J. AND IGUE, J. (1993) 'Market Driven Integration in the Eastern Subregion: Nigeria's Impact on Its Neighbours', Synthesis Report, INRA/IRAM/UNB.

ELLIS, FRANK (1998) 'Survey Article: Household Strategies and Rural Livelihood Diversification', *Journal of Development Studies*, 35(1), 1-38.

ELLIS, FRANK (2000) 'The Determinants of Rural Livelihood Diversification in Developing Countries', *Journal of Agricultural Economics*, 51(2), 289-302.

EVANS, H.E. & NGAU, P. (1991) 'Rural-Urban Relations, Household Income Diversification and Agricultural Productivity', *Development & Change* 22, 519-45.

FISHER, THOMAS, MAHAJAN, VIJAY, AND SINGHA, ASHOK (1997) *The Forgotten Sector. Non-farm employment and enterprises in rural India*. London: Intermediate Technology Publications.

FORREST, TOM (1994) *The Advance of African Capital: The growth of Nigerian private enterprise*. Edinburgh: Edinburgh University Press.

GORDON, ANN (1999) 'Diversity in Rural Incomes: Issues Affecting Access at the Household Level', Paper presented to World Bank/DFID Workshop on Non-Farm Rural Sector and Poverty Alleviation, June 9-10.

GRANOVETTER, MARK (1985) 'Economic Action and Social Structure: The Problem of Embeddedness', *American Journal of Sociology* 91.

GREGOIRE, E. (1991) 'Les chemins de la contrebande: tude des réseaux commerciaux en pays haussa', *Cahiers d'études africaines* 124 XXXI (4), 509-532.

GUYER, JANE AND IDOWU, O. (1991) 'Women's agricultural work in a multi-modal rural economy: Ibarapa District, Oyo State, Nigeria', in C.H. Gladwin, ed., *Structural Adjustment and African Women Farmers*. Gainsville: University of Florida Press.

HAGGBLADE, S., HAZELL, P. AND BROWN, J. (1989) 'Farm-Nonfarm Linkages in Rural Sub-Saharan Africa, *World Development* 17(8), 1173-1201.

HARRISS, BARBARA (1987) 'Regional Growth Linkages from Agriculture', *Journal of Development Studies* 23(2), 275-289.

HART, G. (1994) 'The Dynamics of Diversification in an Asian Rice Region', in B. Koppel et al., eds., *Development or Deterioration?: Work in Rural Asia*, 47-71.

HASHIM, Y. AND MEAGHER, K. (1999) *Cross Border Trade and the Parallel Currency Market: The Organization of Trade and Finance in the Context of Structural Adjustment*. Uppsala: Nordiska Afrikainstitutet, Research Report No. 113.

176

HAZELL, P. & HAGGBLADE S. (1991) 'Rural-Urban Growth Linkages in India', *Indian Journal of Agricultural Economics* 46 (4), 515-529.

HEYER, JUDITH (1996) 'The Complexities of Rural Poverty in Sub-Saharan Africa', *Oxford Development Studies*, 24(3), 281-297.

HILL, P. (1969) 'Hidden Trade in Hausaland', *Man* 4 392-409.

HILL, P. (1972) *Rural Hausa: A village and a setting*. Cambridge: Cambridge University Press.

HILL, P. (1977) *Population, prosperity and poverty: Rural Kano 1900 and 1970*. London: Cambridge University Press.

ILIYA, M. AND SWINDELL, K. (1997) 'Winners and Losers: Household fortunes in the urban peripheries of Northwest Nigeria', in Deborah Bryceson and Vali Jamal, eds. *Farewell to Farms: De-Agrarianization and Employment in Africa*. Aldershot: Ashgate.

IMAM, A. (1993) '"If You Won't Do These Things For Me, I Won't Do Seclusion For You": Local and Regional Constructions of Seclusion Ideologies and Practices in Kano, Northern Nigeria', unpublished D.Phil Thesis, Department of Social Anthropology, University of Sussex.

JACKSON, C. (1985) *The Kano River Irrigation Project' Women's Roles and Gender Differences in Development: Cases for Planners*. West Hartford: Kumarian Press.

JAMAL, V. AND WEEKS, J. (1993) *Africa Misunderstood*. Basingstoke: Macmillian.

KTARDA (1989) 'Crop and Weather Reports', Ajiwa Zonal Office, Ajiwa: Katsina Agricultural and Rural Development Agency.

KTARDA (1993) '1992 Report on Research/Extension Activities in Katsina State'. Katsina: Katsina Agricultural and Rural Development Agency.

LANJOUW, PETER (1999) 'The Rural Non-Farm Sector: A Note on Policy Options', Paper presented to World Bank/DFID Workshop on Non-Farm Rural Sector and Poverty Alleviation, June 9-10.

LIEDHOLM, CARL, MCPHERSON, M. AND CHUTA, E. (1994) 'Small Enterprise Employment Growth in Rural Africa', *American Journal of Agricultural Economics* 76, 1177-1182.

LIEDHOLM, CARL, (1973) 'Research on Employment in the Rural Non-Farm Sector', African Rural Employment Paper No. 5, Department of Agricultural Economics, Michigan State University, Michigan.

LENNIHAN, LOUISE (1987) "Agricultural Wage Labour in Northern Nigeria", in M. Watts, ed., *State, Oil and Agriculture in Nigeria*. Berkeley, California: Institute of International Studies.

LENNIHAN, LOUISE (1994) 'Structural Adjustment and Agricultural Wage Labour in Northern Nigeria: A Preliminary Research Note', Paper presented at the 37th Annual Meeting of the African Studies Association, Toronto, Canada, 3-6 November.

LLAMBI, LUIS (2000) 'Global-Local Links in Latin America's New Ruralities', in Deborah Bryceson, Cristobal Kay and Jos Mooij, eds., *Disappearing Peasantries? Rural Labour in Africa, Asia and Latin America*. London: Intermediate Technology Publications.

LONGHURST, RICHARD (1985) 'Farm Level Decision Making, Social Structure and An Agricultural Development Project in a Northern Nigerian Village', Samaru Miscellaneous Paper 106, IAR.

LOVEJOY, PAUL (1980) *Caravans of Kola, The Hausa Kola Trade: 1700-1900*. Zaria: Ahmadu Bello University Press.

LUBECK, PAUL (1987) 'Islamic Protest and Oil-Based Capitalism: Agriculture, Rural Linkages, and Urban Popular Movements in Northern Nigeria', in M. Watts, ed., *State, Oil and Agriculture in Nigeria*. Berkeley: Institute of International Studies, University of California.

MATLON, PETER J. (1977) *The Size Distribution, Structure, and Determinants of Personal Incomes Among Farmers in the North of Nigeria*. Ph.D. Thesis, Cornell University.

MATLON, PETER J. (1978) *Income Distribution and Patterns of Expenditure, Savings, and Credit Among Farmers in the North of Nigeria*. Occasional Paper 96, Department of Agricultural Economics, Cornell University.

MATLON, PETER J. (1979) *Income Distribution Among Farmers in Northern Nigeria: Empirical Results and Policy Implications*. East Lansing: Michigan State University, African Rural Economy Paper 18.

MATLON, PETER J. (1991) 'Farmer Risk Management Strategies: The Case of the West African Semi-arid Tropics', in D. Holden, P. Hazell, and A. Prichard, eds., *Risk in agriculture: Proceedings of the tenth agriculture sector symposium*, Washington, D.C.: World Bank, 51-79.

MCCORMICK, D. AND PEDERSEN, P. O., eds. (1996) *Small Enterprises: Flexibility and Networking in an African Context* Nairobi: Longhorn Kenya.

MEAGHER, K. (1991) 'Priced Out of the Market: The Effect of Market Liberalization and Parallel Trade on Smallholder Incomes in Northern Nigeria', McNamara Fellowship Report.

MEAGHER, K. (1994) 'Regional Complementarities or Policy Disparities? Cross-Border Trade and Food Security Among Nigeria and Her Sahellian and Coastal Neighbours', in G.A. Obiazor et al., eds., *West African Regional Economic Integration: Nigerian Policy Perspectives in the 1990s*. Lagos: Nigerian Institute of International Affairs.

MEAGHER, K. (1995) 'Parallel Trade and Powerless Places: Research Traditions and Local Realities in Rural Northern Nigeria', *Africa Development* XX(2), 5-19.

MEAGHER, K. (1997) 'Shifting the Imbalance: The Impact of Structural Adjustment on Rural-Urban Population Movements in Northern Nigeria', *Journal of Asian and African Studies* 32(1-2) June.

MEAGHER, K. (1999) 'The Invasion of the Opportunity Snatchers: The Rural-Urban Interface in Northern Nigeria', paper presented at workshop on 'Between Town and Country: Livelihoods, Settlement and Identity Formation in Sub-Saharan Africa', June 27-30, Rhodes University, East London Campus.

MEAGHER, K. (2000) 'Veiled Conflicts: Gender, Differentiation and Structural Adjustment in Nigerian Hausaland', in Deborah Bryceson, Cristobal Kay and Jos Mooij, eds., *Disappearing Peasantries? Rural Labour in Africa, Asia and Latin America*. London: Intermediate Technology Publications.

MEAGHER, K. AND MUSTAPHA, A.R. (1997) 'Not by Farming Alone: The Role of Non-Farm Incomes in Rural Hausaland', in D. Bryceson and V. Jamal, eds., *Farewell to Farms: De-Agrarianization and Employment in Africa*. Aldershot: Ashgate.

MEAGHER, K. AND OGUNWALE, S.A. (1994) "The Grain Drain: The Impact of Cross-Border Grain Trade on Agricultural Production in Northern Nigeria", Research Report for IRAM/INRA/LARES Project on the Eastern Sub-Market (Nigeria and neighbouring countries).

MEAGHER, K., OGUNWALE, S.A., AHMED, B., SANNI, S.A., ABDULSALAM, Z. AND OMOLEHIN, R. (1996) 'Grains and Losses: Recent Developments in the Cross-Border Grain Trade between Nigeria and Niger', Research Report prepared in collaboration with the Projet Stock de Reserve, Office des Produits Vivriers du Niger, December, 1996.

MEAGHER, K. AND M.-B. YUNUSA (1996) 'Passing the Buck: Structural Adjustment and the Nigerian Urban Informal Sector', Discussion Paper 75, UNRISD, May, 1996.

MORTIMORE, MICHAEL (1989) *Adapting to Drought: Farmers, Famines and Desertification in West Africa*. Cambridge University Press.

MURTON, J. (1999) 'Population growth and poverty in Machakos District, Kenya', *Geographical Journal* 165 (1), 37-46.

MUSTAPHA, A.R. (1990) 'Peasant Differentiation and Politics in Rural Kano, 1900-1987', D.Phil Thesis, Politics Sub-Faculty, Oxford University.

MUSTAPHA, A.R. AND MEAGHER, K. (1992) 'Stress, Adaptation and Resilience in Rural Kano', Paper presented at the SSRC/CODESRIA Workshop on African Agriculture, January 18-21, Dakar, Senegal.

NORMAN, D.W. (1973a) "Economic Analysis of Agricultural Production and Labour Utilization Among the Hausa of the North of Nigeria", African Rural Employment Paper 4, East Lansing: Michigan State University.

NORMAN, D.W. (1973b) 'Rural economy in the Zaria area, with specific reference to agriculture', *Samaru Research Bulletin* 178, IAR, Samaru.

NORMAN, D.W., SIMMONS, E.B. AND HAYS, H.M. (1982) *Farming Systems in the Nigerian Savanna*. Boulder Co: Westview Press.

PEDERSEN, POUL OVE (1997) *Small African Towns – Between Rural Networks and Urban Hierarchies*. Aldershot: Avebury.

RASMUSSEN, J., SCHMITZ, H. & VAN DIJK, M.P. (1992) 'Introduction: Exploring a new Approach to Small-Scle Industry', *IDS Bulletin* 23(3).

REARDON, THOMAS (1997) 'Using Evidence of Household Income Diversification to Inform Study of the Rural Nonfarm Labour Market in Africa', *World Development* 25(5), 735-747.

REARDON, THOMAS, DELGADO, C. AND MATLON, P. (1992) 'Determinants and Effects of Income Diversification Amongst Farm Households in Burkina Faso', *Journal of Development Studies* 28(2), 264-296.

REARDON, THOMAS, STAMOULIS, K., BALISACAN, A., CRUZ, M., BEREGUE, J., AND BANKS, B. (1998) 'Rural Non-Farm Income in Developing Countries', *The State of Food and Agriculture*, Rome: FAO.

REARDON, THOMAS, TAYLOR, J.E., STAMOULIS, K., LANJOUW, P., AND BALISACAN, A. (2000) 'Effects of Non-Farm Employment on Rural Income Inequality in Developing Countries: An Investment Perspective', *Journal of Agricultural Economics,* 51(2), 266-288.

ROSS, P. (1987) "Land as a Right to Membership: Land Tenure Dynamics in a Peripheral Area of the Kano Close-Settled Zone", in M. Watts ed., *State, Oil and Agriculture in Nigeria*. Berkeley: Institute of International Studies.

SAHN, DAVID E. AND SARRIS, ALEXANDER (1991) 'Structural Adjustment and the Welfare of Rural Smallholders: A comparative Analysis from Sub-Saharan Africa', *The World Bank Economic Review* 5(2), 259-289.

SAITH, ASHWANI (1992) *The Rural Non-Farm Economy: Processes and Policies*. Geneva: ILO.

SCOONES, IAN (1998) 'Sustainable Rural Livelihoods: A Framework for Analysis', IDS Working Paper 72, Institute of Development Studies, University of Sussex, Brighton.

SIMMONS, E.B. (1975) 'The Small-Scale Rural Food-Processing Industry in Northern Nigeria', *Food Research Institute Studies* 14(2), 147-161.

SIMMONS, E.B. (1990) 'Women in Rural Development in Northern Nigeria', in O. Otite and C. Okali, eds., *Readings in Nigerian Rural Society and Economy* Ibadan: Heinemann.

TIFFEN, MARY, MORTIMORE, M., AND GICHUKI, F. (1994) *More People, Less Erosion: Environmental Recovery in Kenya*. Chichester: John Wiley.

VAN DIJK, M. P. VAN AND RABELLOTTI, R., eds. (1997) *Enterprise Clusters and Networks in Developing Countries*. London: Frank Cass.

WALLACE, T. (1978) "The Concept of Gandu: How Useful Is It In Understanding Labour Relations in Rural Hausa Society?", *Savanna* 7(2), 137-50.

WATTS, MICHAEL, ed. (1987) *State, Oil and Agriculture in Nigeria* Berkeley, California: Institute of International Studies.

WATTS, MICHAEL (1983) *Silent Violence*. Berkeley: University of California Press.

WILLIAMS, GAVIN (1988) "Why is there no agrarian capitalism in Nigeria", *Journal of Historical Sociology* 1(4), December, 345-398.

WORLD BANK (1989) *Sub-Saharan Africa: From Crisis to Sustainable Growth*. New York: Oxford University Press.

WORLD BANK (1978) *Rural Enterprise and Non Farm Employment.* Washington D.C.

YUNUSA, M.-B. (1997) 'Peasant Alliance, Economic Crises and Structural Adjustment in Nigeria: Implications for Rural Development', Centre for Social and Economic Research, Ahmadu Bello University, Zaria, mimeo.

ASC Research Series
published by Ashgate Publishing Ltd.

1. Dick Foeken & Nina Tellegen 1994 — Tied to the land. Living conditions of labourers on large farms in Trans Nzoia District, Kenya

2. Tom Kuhlman 1994 — Asylum or aid? The economic integration of Ethiopian and Eritrean refugees in the Sudan

3. Kees Schilder 1994 — Quest for self-esteem. State, Islam and Mundang ethnicity in Northern Cameroon

4. Johan A. van Dijk 1995 — Taking the waters. Soil and water conservation among settling Beja nomads in Eastern Sudan

5. Piet Konings, 1995 — Gender and class in the tea estates of Cameroon

6. Thera Rasing 1995 — Passing on the rites of passage. Girls' initiation rites in the context of an urban Roman Catholic community on the Zambian Copperbelt

7. Jan Hoorweg, Dick Foeken & Wijnand Klaver, 1995 — Seasons and nutrition at the Kenya coast

8. John A. Houtkamp 1996 — Tropical Africa's emergence as a banana supplier in the inter-war period

9. Victor Azarya 1996 — Nomads and the state in Africa: the political roots of marginality

10. Deborah Bryceson & Vali Jamal, eds., 1997 — Farewell to farms. De-agrarianization and employment in Africa

11. Tjalling Dijkstra 1997 — Trading the fruits of the land: horticultural marketing channels in Kenya

12. Nina Tellegen, 1997 — Rural enterprises in Malawi: necessity or opportunity?

13. Klaas van Walraven 1999 — Dreams of power. The role of the Organization of African Unity in the politics of Africa, 1963-1993

14. Isaac Sindiga 1999 — Tourism and African development. Change and challenge of tourism in Kenya

15. Laurens van der Laan, Tjalling Dijkstra & Aad van Tilburg, eds., 1999 — Agricultural marketing in Tropical Africa. Contributions from the Netherlands

16. Patrick McAllister 2001 — Building the homestead. Agriculture, labour and beer in South Africa's Transkei

Copies can be ordered from:

Ashgate Publishing Direct Sales
Bookpoint Limited
39 Milton Park
Abingdon, Oxon, OX14 4TD
United Kingdom
Fax: +44 (0) 1235 400454
E-mail: orders@bookpoint.co.uk

For Product Safety Concerns and Information please contact our EU
representative GPSR@taylorandfrancis.com Taylor & Francis Verlag GmbH,
Kaufingerstraße 24, 80331 München, Germany

Printed and bound by CPI Group (UK) Ltd, Croydon, CR0 4YY

01/05/2025

01858333-0010